# Everything for Spring

A COLLECTION FROM GRYPHON HOUSE BOOKS

# Everything for Spring

## A Complete Activity Book for Teachers of Young Children

Edited by Kathy Charner
Illustrations by Joan Waites

ACTIVITIES FOR MARCH, APRIL AND MAY

**gryphon house**
Beltsville, Maryland

Published by Gryphon House, Inc.
10726 Tucker Street, Beltsville, MD 20705

World Wide Web: http://www.ghbooks.com

Text Illustrations: Joan Waites

Library of Congress Cataloging-in-Publication Data

Everything for spring  :  a complete activity book for teachers of young
    children  :  activities for March, April, and May  /  edited  by Kathy
    Charner.
        p.    cm.
      "A collection from Gryphon House books."
      Includes bibliographical references and index.
      ISBN 0-87659-187-X  (pbk.)
        1.  Early childhood education--Activity programs.    2.  Early
    childhood education--Curricula.    3.  Spring.    I.  Charner, Kathy.
    II.  Title:  Complete activity book for teachers of young children.
    LB1139.35.A37E847    1997
    372.21--DC21                                                97-21463
                                                                    CIP

# Spring
# Table of Contents

table of contents

# May

# Introduction

Ever wish you could have the advice and suggestions of early childhood experts at your fingertips? It's in this book. With expertise in language, science, math, art, circle and group time, music, transitions and much more, this book gives you just what you need when you need it, in an easy-to-use format. This book contains activities, ideas and suggestions from the following time-tested books:

*500 Five Minute Games*
*Earthways*
*Hug a Tree*
*More Mudpies to Magnets*
*More Story S-t-r-e-t-c-h-e-r-s*
*Mudpies to Magnets*
*One Potato, Two Potato, Three Potato, Four*
*Preschool Art*
*Story S-t-r-e-t-c-h-e-r-s*
*The Complete Learning Center Book*
*The Giant Encyclopedia of Circle Time and Group Activities*
*The Giant Encyclopedia of Theme Activities for Children 2 to 5*
*The Instant Curriculum*
*The Learning Circle*
*The Outside Play and Learning Book*
*The Peaceful Classroom*
*ThemeStorming*
*Transition Time*
*Where Is Thumbkin?*

## Activities appropriate for children

This book is chock-full of activities that teachers have used successfully with children for years. Teachers enjoy the activities because they are appropriate for children and because they are easy to do. Children enjoy the activities because they are fun and filled with things to learn. Whether you teach younger children or older children, or children who have difficulty understanding science concepts or those who need just a little extra help mastering language skills, there is something for you in this book.

## A complete plan

Use this book to plan a morning, a day, a week, a month of activities, a whole season, or, with all three books, a whole school year. There are both teacher-directed and child-directed activities in the book. So while most of the children are independently exploring activities, the teacher can work with one or a few children who have expressed an interest in a certain area or who need additional work in a specific area.

## A monthly plan

As written, this book offers teachers a complete plan for three months. Use this book to develop a monthly plan for March, April and May, using the variety of activities presented, or open the book to any page when you need an activity to fill a morning, a few hours or just a few minutes. This book offers both possibilities. The short sentence or paragraph that introduces each activity often contains learning objectives, an additional help to teachers for planning.

## Integrated curriculum

Although the activities are drawn from different books, most of the activities in each month are related to certain topics or themes, the thematic threads of each month. Other activities related to the season or month (or because they were too much fun to leave out of the book) are also included in each chapter.

The thematic threads for March are:
    Wind
    Nursery Rhymes
    Gas Station

The thematic threads for April are:
    Rain
    Flowers
    Birds
    Gardening

The thematic threads for May are:
    Animals
    Numbers and Letters
    Parties and Fun

Create your own integrated curriculum that meets the needs and interests of your children by selecting related activities for one day, such as circle time, art and math activities, or plan a whole week of activities about Wind (or Birds or Numbers and Letters or any other thematic thread) that includes activities from all areas of the curriculum.

## The monthly chapters

This book has three chapters; each chapter is a complete month of activities containing the following:

***Fingerplays, songs and poems***—use them during circle time or enjoy them anytime during the day.

***Ideas and suggestions for 2 learning centers***—learning centers are great child-oriented places where children experiment with, create and learn about their world.

***Art activities***—children love to express their thoughts, feelings, accomplishments and discoveries through art. The activities focus on the process of art, not the product.

***Circle time and group activities***—activities for the times when all your wonderful individual children are learning to be part of a larger group. These activities, as with most of the activities in the book, are related to the month or the thematic threads of the month.

***Dramatic play activities***—children need little encouragement in this area. Just set up these activities, and let the children play!

***Language activities***—language acquisition, prereading skills and expressive language are just a few of the language skills children learn with these activities.

***Math activities***—activities that are fun, easy-to-do and appropriate for young children. The activities build a conceptual base to help children understand beginning math concepts.

***Music and movement activities***—children love to sing and move. Activities include old favorites and suggestions to turn old favorites into new favorites. Additionally, unique activities to encourage children to get up, move around and learn what their bodies can do are included in this section.

***Science activities***—filled with hands-on activities to help children begin to answer the many "why" questions and learn science skills of estimation, scientific method, problem solving, cause and effect relationships and lots more.

***Snack and cooking activities***—children love cooking projects—experimenting with ingredients, then proudly serving the result to the other children. Activities range from simple recipes with a few ingredients to those requiring more time and ingredients. Children will love them all!

***Transition activities***—ever wonder how to get a child who is engrossed in sand play ready for snack? Or clean up before circle time? Or get a group of children to come inside after outdoor play? Or to settle down to hear a story? This section is filled with tried-and-true activities.

***Games***—enjoy a fun time with a few children or the whole group. Play a game to help children learn math skills, coordination, language skills, listening skills, kindness or cooperation.

***Suggested books***—filled with books children and teachers love that are related to the season or the thematic threads of the month.

***Recommended records and tapes***—filled with records or tapes of songs that children and teachers love and that are related to the season or the thematic threads of the month.

## The activities in each chapter

The activities in each chapter (month) contain the following:

***Title of activity and suggested age***—The title and suggested age tell what the activity is about and the ages most likely to enjoy and learn from the activity.
Note: Individual teachers are the best judges of children in their care. The ages are meant as a suggestion only.

**Short introduction**—This short sentence or paragraph describes the activity, suggests a learning objective or a combination of both.

**Words to use**—Language skills and vocabulary acquisition are developing rapidly in young children. Use this list of words while doing the activity, when talking about what the children will do or when discussing the activity after completion. The words range from simple to complex. Individual teachers will know best which words to introduce and use with their children.

**Materials**—A list of all the materials needed for the activity.

**What to do**—A step-by-step description of each activity. Helpful hints are often included as well as any cautionary notes necessary.

**Want to do more?**—This section includes suggestions for extending the activity using different materials or expanding it into other areas of the curriculum. For example, an art activity might suggest a different material to use instead of paper, or a circle time activity might suggest a related science or math activity.

**Teaching tips**—This section may include specific ways to help children with the activity. For example, a suggestion to tape the paper to the table so it does not move while the child is drawing. Or it may contain suggestions to make the activity simpler for younger children or more complex for older ones. Additionally, this section also may include general tips about working with children such as helping children learn respect for others, reminding teachers that young children get over-stimulated easily and other tips of that nature.

**Home connections**—The connection of home and school is a critical one. Teachers are often looking for ways to help parents feel more connected with what goes on in school. This section contains suggestions of how an activity can be done at home with parents, which may help parents feel more connected to the school or child care facility and help them understand what their child does during the day.

**Books to read and records and tapes**—Suggestions of books, records and tapes that relate to the activity.

# Spring MARCH

# Fingerplays, Poems and Songs

## Five Little Kites

1, 2, 3, 4, 5 little kites,
Flying up in the sky
Said "Hi" to the clouds as they passed by.
Said "Hi" to the birds,
Said "Hi" to the sun.
Said "Hi" to the airplanes,
Oh, what fun!
Then, swish, went the wind,
And they all took a dive.
1, 2, 3, 4, 5.

★ TRANSITION TIME

## I Know a Little Pussy

I know a little pussy; her coat is silver gray.
She lives down in the meadow not very far
   away.
Although she is a pussy, she'll never be a cat,
For she's a pussy willow. What do you think of
   that?
Meow, meow, meow, meow, meow, meow,
   meow!

★ ONE POTATO, TWO POTATO, THREE POTATO, FOUR

## Humpty Dumpty

Humpty Dumpty sat on a wall,
Humpty Dumpty had a great fall;
All the King's horses and all the king's men
Could not put Humpty together again.

★ ONE POTATO, TWO POTATO, THREE POTATO, FOUR

## Little Boy Blue

Little Boy Blue, come blow your horn.
The sheep are in the meadow, the cow's in the
   corn.
But where is the boy who looks after the sheep?
He's under a haystack, fast asleep.

★ ONE POTATO, TWO POTATO, THREE POTATO, FOUR

## Muffin Man

Oh, do you know the muffin man,
The muffin man, the muffin man?
Oh, do you know the muffin man,
Who lives in Drury Lane?

Oh, yes, we know the muffin man,
The muffin man, the muffin man.
Oh, yes, we know the muffin man,
Who lives in Drury Lane.

★ WHERE IS THUMBKIN?

# Jack and Jill

Jack and Jill went up the hill,
To fetch a pail of water;
Jack fell down and broke his crown,
And Jill came tumbling after.

Up Jack got and home did trot,
As fast as he could caper,
Went to bed and bound his head
With vinegar and brown paper.

★ Where Is Thumbkin?

# Mary Had a Little Lamb

Mary had a little lamb,
Little lamb, little lamb,
Mary had a little lamb,
Its fleece was white as snow.

And everywhere that Mary went,
Mary went, Mary went,
And everywhere that Mary went,
The lamb was sure to go.

It followed her to school one day,
School one day, school one day,
It followed her to school one day,
Which was against the rule.

It made the children laugh and play,
Laugh and play, laugh and play,
It made the children laugh and play,
To see a lamb at school.

★ Where Is Thumbkin?

# London Bridge

London Bridge is falling down,
Falling down, falling down,
London Bridge is falling down,
My fair lady.

Build it up with iron bars,
Iron bars, iron bars,
Build it up with iron bars,
My fair lady.

Iron bars will bend and break....
Build it up with pins and needles....
Pins and needles will rust and bend....
Build it up with gravel and stone....
Gravel and stone will wash away....

★ Where Is Thumbkin?

# I'm a Little Teapot

I'm a little teapot,
Short and stout,
Here is my handle,
Here is my spout.
When I get all steamed up,
Hear me shout,
Just tip me over and pour me out.

★ Where Is Thumbkin?

# March Learning Centers

## Gas Station and Garage Center

**While playing in the Gas Station and Garage Center children learn:**
1. To expand their vocabulary as they use words related to transportation and automotive services.
2. To develop an understanding of workers in the community and appreciate their special abilities.
3. To develop social skills while working with others on cooperative projects in the center.
4. To increase their fine motor coordination as they work on tasks.

**Suggested props for the Gas Station and Garage Center**
tools in a tool box such as
    wrench
    screw driver
    pliers
    measuring tape
    tire gauge
cash register
blocks and planks (used to construct
    a car ramp)
flashlights
plastic bucket containing
    sponges, spray bottles, paper
    towels and squeegee blades
tricycles, wagons, toy cars and
    trucks to be repaired
small tires
pieces of clear plumbing hose
    and funnels of different sizes
empty cans with labels: oil, antifreeze,
    wax
dress-up clothes for role playing: coveralls, gloves, caps and
    goggles
cloths for cleaning and wiping hands and for oil changes
play money

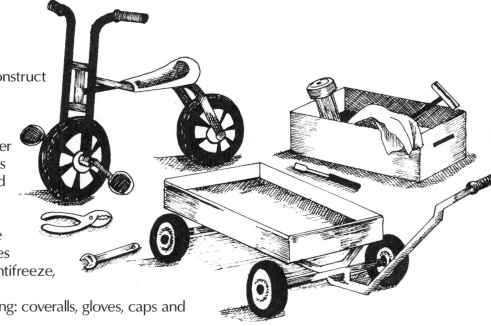

## Curriculum Connections

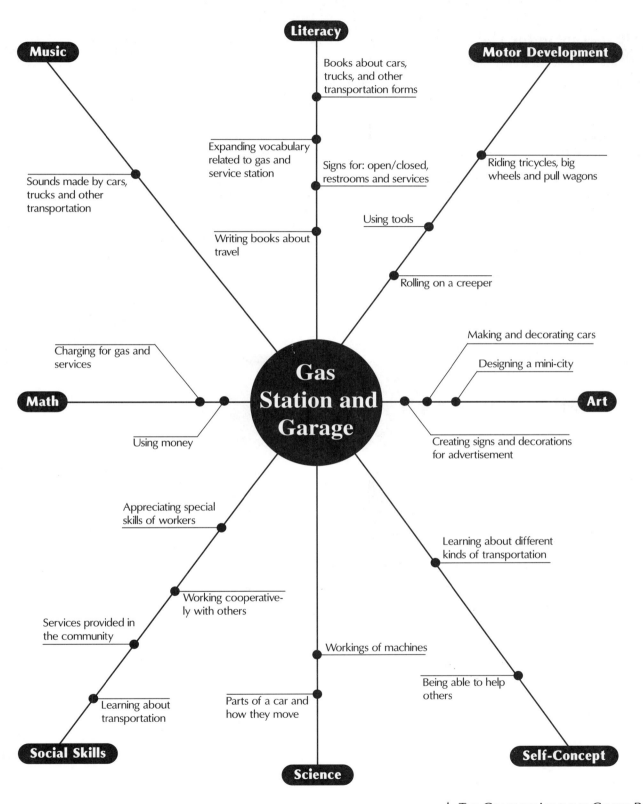

**Literacy**

Books about cars, trucks, and other transportation forms

Expanding vocabulary related to gas and service station

Signs for: open/closed, restrooms and services

Writing books about travel

**Music**

Sounds made by cars, trucks and other transportation

**Motor Development**

Riding tricycles, big wheels and pull wagons

Using tools

Rolling on a creeper

**Math**

Charging for gas and services

Using money

**Art**

Making and decorating cars

Designing a mini-city

Creating signs and decorations for advertisement

**Gas Station and Garage**

Appreciating special skills of workers

Working cooperatively with others

Services provided in the community

Learning about transportation

Learning about different kinds of transportation

Workings of machines

Being able to help others

Parts of a car and how they move

**Social Skills**

**Science**

**Self-Concept**

★ THE COMPLETE LEARNING CENTER BOOK

# Hat Center

## While playing in the Hat Center children learn:

1. To take on roles and participate in play sequences.
2. To develop small motor skills as they make hats in the center.
3. To enhance their creativity as they use their imagination and flexible thinking in the Hat Center.
4. To enjoy new stories about hats and retell them in the center.

## Suggested props for the hat center

Books related to the Hat Center, such as
*Aunt Flossie's Hats (and Crab Cakes Later)*
   by Elizabeth Howard
*Caps for Sale* by Esphyr Slobodkina
*Ho for a Hat!* by William J. Smith
*Jennie's Hat* by Ezra Jack Keats
*Martin's Hats* by Joan W. Blos
many different kinds of hats
   (Be sure to include hats that are worn by
   men and women. Hats of community
   helpers such as fire fighters or police offi-
   cers add variety to the collection.)
a low table
materials needed for making hats, such as

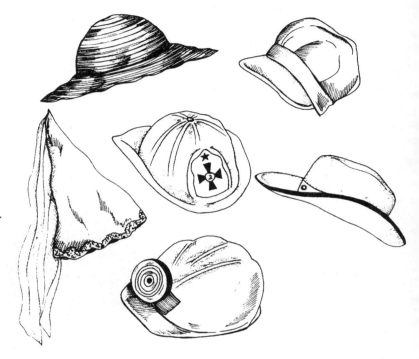

| | |
|---|---|
| newspaper | large pieces |
| scraps of fabric |   of paper |
| glue | tape |
| stapler | scissors |
| foil | feathers |
| trim | net |
| buttons | yarn |
| glitter | pipe cleaners |
| bubble paint | metallic contact paper pieces |
| markers | |

child-size dolls
mirror
cash register
hat boxes
low coat tree for hats

## Curriculum Connections

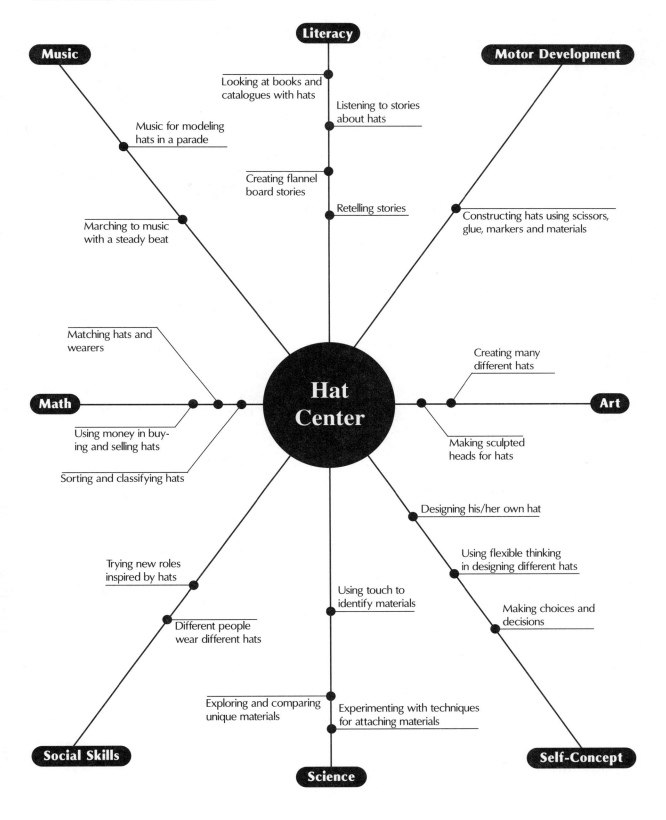

**Music**

Music for modeling hats in a parade

Marching to music with a steady beat

**Literacy**

Looking at books and catalogues with hats

Listening to stories about hats

Creating flannel board stories

Retelling stories

**Motor Development**

Constructing hats using scissors, glue, markers and materials

**Math**

Matching hats and wearers

Using money in buying and selling hats

Sorting and classifying hats

**Hat Center**

Creating many different hats

**Art**

Making sculpted heads for hats

Designing his/her own hat

Using flexible thinking in designing different hats

Making choices and decisions

**Social Skills**

Trying new roles inspired by hats

Different people wear different hats

Using touch to identify materials

Exploring and comparing unique materials

Experimenting with techniques for attaching materials

**Self-Concept**

**Science**

★ THE COMPLETE LEARNING CENTER BOOK

# Art Activities

## Wind Sock

**3+**

*Children learn that the wind blows hard and soft and from different directions.*

### Words to use

cylinder
windy
blow
direction
hard
soft
wind sock
observe
watch

### Materials

paper
markers
stapler
streamers (three 10"
   strips per child)
ribbon (10" per child)

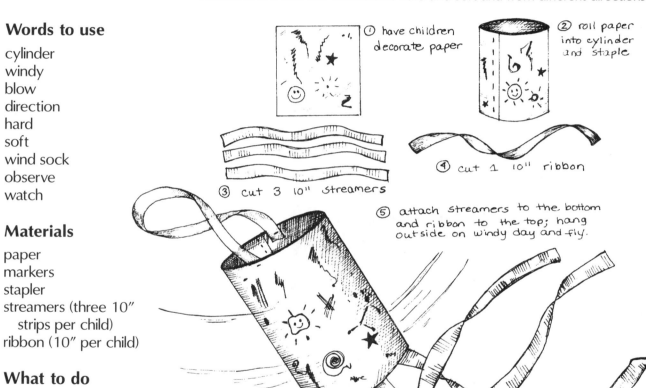

① have children decorate paper
② roll paper into cylinder and staple
③ cut 3 10" streamers
④ cut 1 10" ribbon
⑤ attach streamers to the bottom and ribbon to the top; hang outside on windy day and fly.

### What to do

1. Ask the children to decorate their papers using markers.
2. Roll each paper into a cylinder and staple it.
3. Attach the streamers to the bottom of the cylinder.
4. Attach a ribbon to the top for hanging.
5. On a windy day, hang the wind socks outside where the children can observe them. Perhaps leave them up for several days, so they can see how the wind changes over time. Talk about the direction the wind is blowing and whether it is blowing hard or soft.

### Want to do more?

Allow children to take their wind socks home and observe them for a longer period of time.

★ The Giant Encyclopedia of Theme Activities

# Mad Hatters

*Children create hats to use in their play.*

## Words to use

baskets        hat
decorate      ribbon

## Materials

baskets
ribbons, flowers and beads

## What to do

1. Provide a variety of baskets, ribbons, flowers and beads.
2. Encourage children to invert baskets and decorate them to make hats.
3. Children's' interest may be stimulated by reading *Jennie's Hat* by Ezra Jack Keats.

★ THE INSTANT CURRICULUM

# Colonial Hat

3+

*Children learn how to make a hat that can be used in their play.*

## Words to use

circle
stitch
fabric

## Materials

white fabric or crepe paper
scissors
yarn and plastic needles

## What to do

1. Help children make a colonial hat by cutting circles out of white fabric or crepe paper.
2. With yarn and large plastic needles, the children sew stitches around the fabric piece, about two inches from the edge.

① punch holes around the edge of a large circle of fabric, children sew stiches around the fabric.

② The yarn is pulled to gather the stitches and tied in a bow.

3. When they have completed their sewing, the teacher helps the children gather the stitches together to produce the hat.
4. Secure the yarn by tying.

★ THE COMPLETE LEARNING CENTER BOOK

art activities

MARCH

# Three-Cornered Hat

**3+**

*Children learn to make a hat that can be used in their play.*

## Words to use

three
staple
strip

## Materials

construction paper
scissors
stapler or tape

## What to do

1. Draw lines on construction paper approximately three inches wide and four inches long.
2. The children cut out the strips.
3. Help the children staple or tape three strips together on each end to produce a triangle shaped, three cornered hat.
4. Vary the length of the strips to fit the size of the child's head.

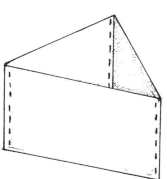

3" × 4"
① children cut 3 strips of paper 3" × 4"

② staple all three strips together, vary the length of the strips to fit each child's head.

③ decorate with paint, stickers, and assorted craft items

★ THE COMPLETE LEARNING CENTER BOOK

# Bonnets

**3+**

*Spring is a great time to make these hats.*

## Words to use

punch          chin
decorate       bonnet

## Materials

paper plate
hole punch
string or elastic
decorative items such as ribbon, lace, fabric scraps, beads, artificial flowers,
    bows, felt scraps, streamers, confetti or glitter
crayons, felt pens or paints
glue

## What to do

1. With adult help, punch a hole on each side of the paper plate. Tie pieces of string through the holes to make a chin strap to hold the bonnet in place when it is complete.
2. Turn the plate upside down on the table.
3. Begin attaching decorations and collage items to the plate to create a bonnet. Use crayons or pens to further decorate the bonnet.
4. Keep the underside of the hat plain for easier handling. If decorating the underside is desired, ask the artist to do this before decorating the top of the bonnet.
5. Dry the bonnet thoroughly and then wear it.

## Want to do more?

Play music and have the artists march in a bonnet parade. Use only tissue scraps, doilies and foil for a daintier design. Create a "theme" bonnet, such as the environment, favorites foods, pets.

## Teaching tips

Use one piece of elastic attached to both holes of the bonnet. Measure the elastic from one side of the bonnet, under the child's chin, to the other side of the bonnet. No tying necessary!

★ PRESCHOOL ART

# Fancy Hats                                    3+

*Children learn to make a hat that can be used in their play.*

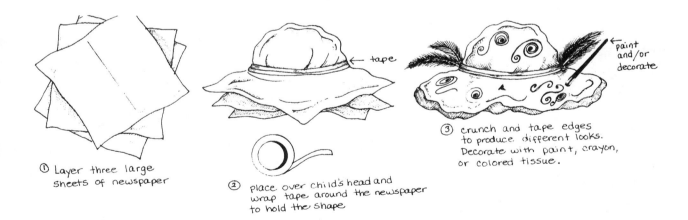

① Layer three large sheets of newspaper

② place over child's head and wrap tape around the newspaper to hold the shape

← tape

③ crunch and tape edges to produce different looks. Decorate with paint, crayon, or colored tissue.

paint and/or decorate

## Words to use

| | |
|---|---|
| newsprint | make |
| form | construct |
| brim | custom |

## Materials

newsprint
masking tape
flowers, glitter, feathers, fabric, etc.
glue and tape

## What to do

1. Place a sheet of newsprint on a child's head.
2. Make the hat crown by wrapping masking tape around the paper to the form of the child's head, assuring a custom fit.
3. Roll the edges of the paper to produce a brim.
4. The children decorate the finished construction with flowers, glitter, feathers, net, fabric, braid or other materials from the work table.

★ THE COMPLETE LEARNING CENTER BOOK

# Jack and Jill                                      3+

*A fun way to learn the rhyme "Jack and Jill"!*

## Words to use

rhyme
hill
tumble
fall down
crown

## Materials

construction paper
Exacto knife (for teacher!)
glue
crayons
craft sticks

exacto knife to cut slit (for teacher!)

5"

add grass and flowers to the hill; draw a well at the top of each hill.

## What to do

1. Draw a hill, and cut a 5" vertical slit in the center of the hill. Repeat for each child.
2. The children use crayons to add tufts of grass or flowers to the hills.
3. Draw a well at the top of each hill.
4. Children draw faces and clothing on Jack and Jill.
5. Attach Jack and Jill to craft sticks.
6. Move Jack and Jill up and down the hill as you recite the rhyme.

## Want to do more?

Have children imagine other things that Jack and Jill could fetch at the top of the hill, for example, gravel, flowers, fruit, leaves, etc.

★ THE GIANT ENCYCLOPEDIA OF THEME ACTIVITIES

# Plaster Bag Art                                    3+

*A neat and tidy way to make a plaster of Paris sculpture.*

## Words to use

| | |
|---|---|
| plaster | sculpture |
| shape | dough |
| harden | scoop |
| set | mix |
| wet and soft | dry and hard |

## Materials

plaster of Paris
water
plastic sandwich bag
powdered tempera paints
liquid tempera paints, optional
paintbrushes, optional
wooden block or piece of matte board for a base, optional

## What to do

1. Scoop some plaster of Paris into a plastic sandwich bag. Add a tablespoon or more of powdered tempera paint to the plaster. Add some water to form a soft dough.
2. Squeeze the plastic bag with the hands to mix the water, paint and plaster. When the plaster feels warm to the touch, it is beginning to set and will set quickly.
3. Hold the bag in any desired shape as the plaster hardens.
4. When the sculpture is hard, remove it from the bag.
5. Paint further with liquid tempera paint, if desired.
6. Glue the sculpture to a wooden block or piece of matte board for a base, if desired.

## Teaching tips

Experiment with the measurements of plaster and water before trying this with young artists. Measurements can vary from day to day, but a half bag of plaster and a quarter cup of water is a good start.

★ PRESCHOOL ART

# Muffin Holder Flowers

**3+**

*Children create flowers from paper muffin holders.*

**Words to use**

flower
stems
leaves

**Materials**

paper muffin/cupcake holders
construction paper
glue
crayons

**What to do**

1. Use paper muffin/cupcake holders for flower faces. Different-sized cupcake holders make different-sized flowers.
2. Glue them on construction paper and use crayons to add stems, leaves and backgrounds.

★ WHERE IS THUMBKIN?

# Straw Blowing

**3+**

*Try this unique "paintbrush"!*

**Words to use**

paint
blow
straw

**Materials**

spoon
tempera paint
paper
straws
scissors

**What to do**

1. Use a spoon to place a small amount of tempera paint on each child's paper.
2. Give each child a straw (a cut-in-half straw is easier to handle).
3. Allow children to blow through the straw to move paint across the paper and create a design.
Note: Be sure children blow out and not in!

★ THE INSTANT CURRICULUM

# Spring Mud Painting

*Playing in mud is fun! This activity brings the fun and creative experience indoors.*

## Words to use

dirt
mud
squish

## Materials

presifted dirt or potting soil
water
empty ice cream pails or large containers for mixing mud
large spoons for mixing, measuring cups and spoons
newspaper
fingerpaint paper or freezer paper
aprons or paint smocks

## What to do

1. Cover the work surface and have children put on paint smocks or aprons. Divide children into small groups. Supply each group with a spoon, pail with dirt and measuring cup with water. Give each child a sheet of paper.
2. Each group works together to mix their own mud and then fingerpaints with it. Let the mud air dry completely and display.
3. Allow time for the children to share their feelings and observations about the mud paintings. Everyone who participates can help clean up.

## Want to do more?

Do the entire activity outdoors and allow the children to play more extensively with the mud. Measure the amounts of dirt and water used and write out a mud "recipe." Use utensils instead of fingers to make a painting. This may be helpful for those who do not wish to put their hands in the mud.

## Song to sing

"Mud, Mud, Mud Is Fun" (to the tune of "Row, Row, Row Your Boat")

> *Mud, mud, mud is fun.*
> *Watch us stir it up.*
> *Round and round and round and round*
> *Mud is fun to make.*
> *Mud, mud, mud is fun.*
> *Listen to it squish.*
> *Through our fingers, round our toes*
> *Squish is how it goes.*

**Books to read**

*The Mud Pony* by Caron Lee Cohen
*Mud Puddle* by Robert N. Munsch

★ THE GIANT ENCYCLOPEDIA OF THEME ACTIVITIES

# Good Graffiti

# 3+

*What's wet and fun—Good Graffiti!*

## Words to use

draw          chalk
wet           dry

## Materials

chalk

## What to do

On days when the ground is soggy and when children can't play on grass, give them chalk to draw on the sidewalk or patio.

★ THE INSTANT CURRICULUM

# Paper Dolls

# 4+

*Children love to make these dolls.*

## Words to use

collage           clothing
decorate          puppet
accessories       story

## Materials

old file folders
scissors
glue
collage items such as yarn, buttons, beads, beans, lace or felt
pens or crayons

## What to do

1. With adult help, cut old file folders into the shape of a doll body without features or clothing. The shape should be fairly chubby and thick so it will be strong enough to support gluing.
2. Draw or color on the doll shape before decorating further.

3. Begin decorating the doll shape with collage items for hair, eyes, clothing, jewelry, a hat, glasses or other features to dress the doll.

4. Allow the doll the dry completely.

## Want to do more?

Make characters from a favorite story or play such as the gingerbread boy, a farmer, a farmer's wife and a wolf. Make the paper dolls into puppets by taping each one to a dowel or stick so they can be manipulated above a partition or curtain. Removable clothing for the doll can be made from paper or fabric scraps.

## Teaching tips

Young artists tend to use a lot of glue when adding the collage items, so carry the doll flat to a drying area and leave for a day or two. If the doll is carried upright, all the glue and collage items will slide off the doll shape.

cut doll shape from old file folder

Color and decorate doll shape

★ PRESCHOOL ART

# Paper Bag Kite

**5+**

*Children love to make kites!*

## Words to use

reinforce
kite
fly

## Materials

large paper grocery bag
hole punch
paints and brushes
tissue paper
crepe paper
ribbons

string
stick-on paper reinforcement circles
white glue
paper scraps and collage materials
streamers
paper liners for muffin tins or candy cups

## What to do

1. Punch four holes in the paper bag, one on each of the four corners about one-half inch from the edge of the bag. Stick a reinforcement circle on each hole.
2. Cut two pieces of string to about 36 inches in length. Tie each end of one string into a reinforced hole to form a loop. Make a loop with the second string.
3. Cut another piece of string to about 36 inches long. Put it through the two loops and tie it. (This will be the kite handle.)
4. Paint the bag as desired. Allow the paint to dry completely.
5. Glue paper collage materials and streamers to the paper bag kite. Dry the kite completely.
6. Open the bag. Hold onto the string and run. The wind will catch in the bag and the kite will fly out and above the artist.

## Teaching tips

For the strongest and most successful kite experience, the bag must dry completely between painting, decorating and flying. Adult assistance is needed when tying the string to the bag but the decorating and flying is completely child-centered. Add extra reinforcements or clear contact paper to the holes to make the kite last longer.

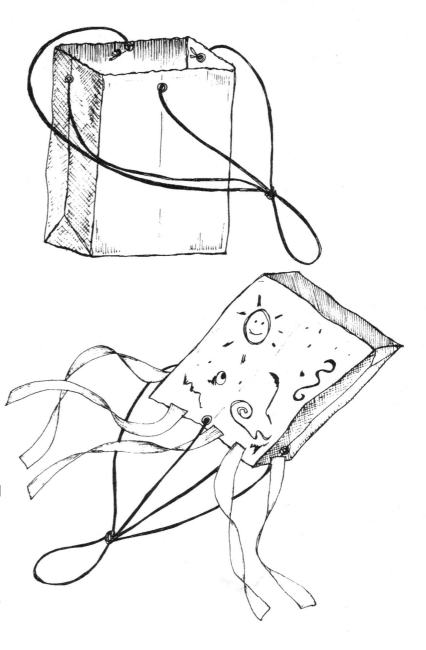

★ PRESCHOOL ART

# Circle Time and Group Activities

## Roll a Rhyme

3+

*A fun way to choose a rhyme.*

### Words to use

roll
cube
die

### Materials

1 empty half-gallon milk carton
construction paper
glue
marker
titles or pictures of 6 songs, fingerplays
    or nursery rhymes

### What to do

1. Construct one large die from the milk carton. Cut off the top of the carton, cut the carton in half and slide one half into the other to form a cube (see illustration).
2. Glue construction paper on all six sides.
3. Draw the title or pictures depicting a song (fingerplay, nursery rhyme) on each side of the cube.
4. Roll the cube (die) and sing the song that shows on top of the die.

### Want to do more?

**Games**: Add other dice games to the classroom. Create other games to play using the die that you made.

★ THE GIANT ENCYCLOPEDIA OF CIRCLE TIME AND GROUP ACTIVITIES

# Miss and Mr. Muffet

**3+**

*Children love to act out this nursery rhyme.*

## Words to use

spider
tuffet
frighten
chair
bowl
spoon
act out
dramatize
run away
pretend
audience

## Materials

chair
plastic bowl and spoon

## What to do

1. At circle time place a chair, a plastic bowl and a spoon in the middle of the circle. Explain that a few of the children will act out the nursery rhyme while the other children say the rhyme and make up the audience.
2. Ask one child to be Miss Muffet or Mr. Muffet and a few children to be the spiders.
3. Miss (Mr.) Muffet sits on the chair with her back to the rest of the children.
4. The spiders get on their knees and begin to crawl toward Miss (Mr.) Muffet as the other children say the nursery rhyme.

> Little Miss (Mr.) Muffet sat on her (his) tuffet, (pretends to eat)
> Eating her (his) curds and whey.
> Along came the spiders and
> Sat down beside her (him), (spiders crawl very close)
> And frightened Miss (Mr.) Muffet away. (drops bowl and spoon and
>    runs away)

5. Vary the dramatization to include several children playing the role of Miss Muffet and only one child pretending to be the spider.

## Want to do more?

**Art:** Provide string, scissors and tape or glue for the children to make spider webs.
**Music:** Sing the "Eensy, Weensy Spider."

★ THE GIANT ENCYCLOPEDIA OF CIRCLE TIME AND GROUP ACTIVITIES

# Humpty Dumpty

*This nursery rhyme is always a favorite.*

## Words to use

wall
fall
back together
crack
rhyme
dramatize
eggs

## Materials

eggs (hard boiled)
markers
forks and plates

## What to do

1. Say the "Humpty Dumpty" nursery rhyme with the children.

> *Humpty Dumpty sat on a wall.*
> *Humpty Dumpty had a great fall.*
> *All the King's horses and all the King's men,*
> *Couldn't put Humpty together again.*

2. Dramatize the rhyme by asking the children to make their hands into two fists touching each other and to pretend that their fists are Humpty Dumpty. Tell the children to pretend that their arms are the wall. At the end of the rhyme ask children to open their fists and spread their fingers to represent the cracked egg.
3. Give each of the children a hard boiled egg and invite the children to draw faces on the eggs. Allow the children to drop their eggs on the floor to see how Humpty Dumpty cracked.
4. Help the children peel the eggs and save the shells to be dyed and used for collage projects. Eat the eggs for snack.
5. Talk about other ways that eggs are prepared and the different foods that contain egg.

## Want to do more?

**Math:** Store a dozen colored cardboard eggs (cut in half) in an egg carton. The children match the halves.
**Science:** Talk about baby animals that hatch from eggs (frogs, chickens, turtles, birds) and the different sizes of the eggs.

## Books to read

*Egg to Chick* by Millicent Selsam
*Horton Hatches an Egg* by Dr. Seuss

★ THE GIANT ENCYCLOPEDIA OF CIRCLE TIME AND GROUP ACTIVITIES

circle time activities

# Billy Goats Gruff

**3+**

*Children love to act out stories.*

### Words to use

bridge
goat
troll

### Materials

masking tape
*The Three Billy Goats Gruff* by Ellen Appleby

### What to do

1. Make a masking tape bridge on the floor. Teacher reads or tells the story of *The Three Billy Goats Gruff* as three children act out the goats walking over the bridge and another child acts out the troll under the bridge.
2. Let children take turns acting out the parts.

★ THE INSTANT CURRICULUM

# Story Headbands

**3+**

*Story dramatizations are a fun way to extend story time or entertain children. Spark their language skills and imaginations with simple costumes and props.*

### Words to use

act out
character
headband
story
narrator
prop
costume

### Materials

sentence strips or poster
    board cut into 3″ x 22″
    strips
scissors
glue
markers
paper clips
construction paper

## What to do

1. Draw the heads of various story characters on construction paper.
2. Color them, cut them out and glue them to the sentence strips or poster board to make headbands.
3. Fit them to the child's head and secure with paper clips.
4. After reading or telling a story to the children, discuss the main characters, the setting and the different events.
5. Let the children choose which characters they would like to be, put on the headbands and act out the story. (For younger children, the teacher will need to be the narrator and give guidance as the story is performed.)
6. If time permits, choose other children and let them act out the story.

## Want to do more?

Let children make their own story headbands for acting out stories, rhymes or songs. Let children make up new endings to old, familiar stories. Glue felt ears, horns and other details to plastic headbands to make story props. Place story props and costumes in the housekeeping area for children to play with.

★ TRANSITION TIME

# Imagination Chair                                    3+

*Children develop imagination and an appreciation for others.*

## Words to use

imagine
What would I do if...

## Materials

chair
cushion and bows, optional

## What to do

1. Decorate a special chair and call it the "Imagination Chair." It could be an adult-sized chair with a pretty cushion and bows.
2. Children take turns sitting in the chair and describing what they would do if they were a certain person of importance or renown. Examples: "If I were a king (or queen), I would...." "If I were an astronaut, I would...." Holiday adaptation: "If I were Santa Claus, I would...."

★ THE INSTANT CURRICULUM

# Spring Hunt

**3+**

*Encourage children to develop observation skills with this activity.*

### Words to use

notice
collect

### Materials

paper bags
felt pen

### What to do

1. Write each child's name on a paper bag.
2. Go for a Spring Hunt outside to observe and collect spring things. Suggested spring things are grass, clover, wild flowers, dandelions, rocks, leaves, twigs or even a ladybug.
3. While the children are collecting spring things have them take a deep breath to experience the smell of spring. Smell the flowers and grass.
4. Notice how a spring day looks from the ground to the sky.
5. Lie down and observe the day from a different angle or crouch down to see it from the perspective of a small animal. The items that are placed in the bags can be taken home and shared.
6. At circle time ask each child to share what he or she has collected. Discuss the various objects noting their color and texture. Imagine what the earth would be like without one of these items.

### Teaching tips

Everyone is eager to share their treasures, but waiting for a turn is difficult. As each child shows an item, the other children can search in their own bags for a similar find. Give each child a different colored sheet of construction paper to place their spring things on. This will help prevent the items from scattering.

★ THE LEARNING CIRCLE

# Spring Mural

**3+**

*Discover all the different aspects of Spring.*

### Words to use

objects          pictures
mural            spring
flowers          grass
butterfly        tree
branch

## Materials

butcher paper
crayons
scissors
magazines
paper
paint
paintbrushes
tape
suggested spring items: paintings by the children, dried flowers, tree bark, branches, leaves, pictures of insects and baby animals and even Easter eggs

## What to do

1. Secure the butcher paper on a wall. Print the word *Spring* on the butcher paper.
2. Attach spring objects and pictures to the butcher paper to create a Spring Mural.
3. Paint flowers, grass and butterflies on the mural.
4. Cut out magazine pictures relating to spring and add them to the mural.
5. Encourage the children to bring spring items from home to put on the mural.
6. At circle time discuss each item on the mural, its importance, and the ways in which it is related to spring.

## Want to do more?

Add something new to the mural. See who can find what it is—a ladybug drawn on a flower or sunflower seeds glued in a corner. Play a guessing game. Describe an object on the mural and see who can guess it correctly. Create a Summer, Winter and Fall Mural that suggests the unique feeling and mood of each season.

## Teaching tips

The degree to which the children become involved is influenced by the enthusiasm of the teacher. Greet each new item as though seeing it for the first time. When discussing the various spring items use a question and answer format. What spring things that fly in the air can go on the mural? Ask for raised hands.

★ THE LEARNING CIRCLE

# Dramatic Play Activities

## Building a Car

**3+**

*Children make a car to use in their play.*

**Words to use**

box
car
drive

**Materials**

large cardboard boxes
scissors
crayons and markers
tempera paint and brushes or colored contact paper

**What to do**

1. Cut cardboard boxes to create cars. (Adult help may be needed with this step.)
2. Let the children paint and decorate them, then drive them to the garage. Encourage each child to design her car in a special way, making each uniquely different.

★ THE COMPLETE LEARNING CENTER BOOK

## Car Wash

**3+**

*Adding water also adds up to lots more fun.*

**Words to use**

wash
soap
scrub
rinse
bucket
soap suds
bubbles
clean
dry

## Materials

hose
wheeled toys
bucket
mild soap
rags and towels

## What to do

1. On a water play day, hook up the hose and let the children wash cars (wheeled toys).
2. Provide buckets of mild soap and rags for washing.
3. Provide large rags or towels for drying.

★ THE INSTANT CURRICULUM

# Drive-In                                3+

*Children learn social skills as they play.*

## Words to use

take-out
order
clerk
customer

## Materials

large appliance box
scissors
Styrofoam boxes
table
cap
wheeled toys

## What to do

1. Obtain a large appliance box.
2. Children draw windows and doors on a box. Adult cuts windows and doors in box.
3. Place the box in the play yard near the wheeled toy path so children can drive in to order.
4. Use Styrofoam boxes for "take-out" orders. Stack on a small table placed in the box.
5. Provide a cap for the "clerk."
6. One child at a time can go in the box and serve the "customers" as they drive by.

★ THE INSTANT CURRICULUM

# Bakery

**3+**

*Children learn creativity, cooperation and negotiation skills.*

### Words to use

bake
bread
cake
cookies
sell

### Materials

props for a bakery—pots, pans, cookie sheets, muffin tins, baker's hat, playdough, pretend money, cookie cutters, etc.

### What to do

1. Set up a bakery in the dramatic play center using any props you can gather.
2. Encourage the children to role-play activities that might happen at the bakery.

★ WHERE IS THUMBKIN?

# Tea Party

**3+**

*Children develop imagination and social skills.*

### Words to use

tea
cups
drink
treats
May I serve you more tea?
please
thank you

### Materials

tea cups and saucers
teapots
table and chairs

### What to do

1. Sit with the children and have a pretend tea party.
2. Ask them to suggest foods to "eat."

★ WHERE IS THUMBKIN?

# Spring Cleaning

*Children participate in the "spring cleaning" of their classroom.*

## Words to use

dust
mop
wash
scrub
sweep
clean out
straighten up

## Materials

housekeeping area
cleaning supplies: rags, washcloths, old
   towels, spray bottles, water, brooms,
   mops, feather duster

## What to do

1. Set up your dramatic play center as a housekeeping area with a stove, a sink, a refrigerator, table and chairs.
2. Put out the cleaning supplies listed above.
3. Begin to clean in the housekeeping area. Encourage the children to join you and allow them to clean windows, sweep and mop floors, wipe and dust shelves, etc. This could expand to cleaning the entire room.
4. Your room is suddenly spic and span!

## Want to do more?

Children could also clean up for visitors, an important holiday, or a special occasion. Clean up outdoors—rake, sweep and pick up trash to help take care of the environment.

## Song to sing

"This Is the Way We Clean" (sung to "Here We Go Round the Mulberry Bush")

> *This is the way we clean our room,*
> *Clean our room, clean our room,*
> *This is the way we clean our room,*
> *Until it's spic and span!*
> *This is the way we sweep our floors, etc.*

★ The Giant Encyclopedia of Theme Activities

# Language Activities

## Positional Words

**3+**

*Children use their bodies to learn about positional words*

### Words to use

under               on top of
beside              on

### Materials

beanbags

### What to do

1. Give each child, or a few children, a beanbag.
2. Ask children to put the beanbag *on* their shoulder, *under* their chin, *beside* their shoe, *on top* of their head, etc.

★ THE INSTANT CURRICULUM

## Writing Rhymes

**3+**

*Children learn that rhyming words are words that sound alike.*

### Words to use

sounds like         rhyme

### Materials

book of nursery rhymes

### What to do

1. Read several simple rhymes for children. Nursery rhymes provide a good example of simple rhymes.
2. Make up a rhyme with the children and write it on a flip chart.
   Examples:

> *Jogging is fun.*
> *If you like to run.*
>
> *Walking is great.*
> *But don't be late.*

★ THE INSTANT CURRICULUM

# Rebus Charts

*Children learn beginning reading skills.*

## Words to use

drawing
noun

## Materials

chart paper and
 markers

## What to do

1. Ask children to recall an experience such as a recent trip or family gathering. Write the experiences of the children on charts and add drawings beside or over certain nouns.

I went to the rodeo and wore my new hat and my new boots.

For example: I went to the rodeo and wore my hat (drawing) and my new boots (drawing).

2. Let children help you "reread" what was written.

★ THE INSTANT CURRICULUM

# Storyteller's Chair

3+

*If half the class has finished cleaning up, washing their hands or has completed another activity, let them entertain each other by telling stories. Storytelling is an old tradition that should be fostered in children. In addition to building oral language, it helps children develop confidence and good listening skills.*

## Words to use

story                    remember
folk tale                book

## Materials

director's chair, stool or other wooden chair
gold or silver spray paint
ribbons, glitter or other trimmings

### What to do

1. Spray the chair with gold or silver spray paint.
2. Write "Storyteller's Chair" on it and decorate with glitter, ribbons, etc.
3. Choose one child to sit in the chair and tell stories to the other children.
4. Stories may be original or the children's own versions of familiar folk tales and books.

### Want to do more?

Let children read (or pretend to read) books to friends as they sit in the chair. Use a storyteller's hat, cape, magic wand or other props to encourage storytelling.

★ TRANSITION TIME

# Transportation                                      3+

*Children learn about different forms of transportation.*

### Words to use

bicycle
motorcycle
car
truck
van
school bus
bus
subway
train
plane

### Materials

pictures and books about different forms of transportation
paper
crayons, markers
tape
stapler

### What to do

1. Include pictures and books about different forms of transportation the children in the classroom use. Examples include van, school bus, truck, bus, motorcycle, station wagon, bicycle, subway, train.
2. The children draw pictures of different forms of transportation.
3. Bind together to create books about the transportation the children use and where they travel.

★ THE COMPLETE LEARNING CENTER BOOK

# Journals

*Journals provide a quiet, independent activity for children as they arrive at school in the morning, after nap or at the end of the day. Children have the opportunity to write, scribble or draw and to express their thoughts and ideas.*

## Words to use

write
draw
journal
book
scribble
think
notebook
thoughts
dictation
remember
recall
pictures
stories

## Materials

spiral ring notebook
pencil, crayons, markers

## What to do

1. Ask each child to bring in a spiral ring notebook.
2. When they come in the morning, let them get their journals and begin to draw or write.
3. Be available to take their dictation.
4. Set aside a special time for the children to share what is in their journals.

## Want to do more?

Save journals throughout the school year as part of the child's assessment portfolio. They tell a story about the child. Use journals at the end of the day for children to recall what they have done at school. Make a different journal for each month. Give the children a piece of construction paper to decorate for the cover. Count out the number of pages they will need and staple them in the book. Make a "Good Book" for each child and let them draw pictures and write stories about good things they do or what they like about themselves.

★ TRANSITION TIME

# Math Activities

## Tall and Short

### 3+

*Children learn sorting skills by sorting tall and short objects.*

**Words to use**

tall
short
sort

**Materials**

pairs of items that are tall and short—tall teapot, short teapot; tall flower, short flower; tall glass, short glass; tall paper towel tube, short toilet paper tube, etc.

**What to do**

Encourage the children to group the items into tall and short categories.

★ WHERE IS THUMBKIN?

## Hard and Soft

### 3+

*Children learn tactile discrimination.*

**Words to use**

hard
soft
sort

**Materials**

a variety of items that are hard (golf ball, spool, crayon, block) and soft (cotton ball, sponge, tissue, sock)
small boxes or baskets

**What to do**

1. Place all the items on the table.
2. Help the children sort hard items into one basket and the soft items into another.

★ WHERE IS THUMBKIN?

# Big and Little Lambs

*This activity helps children learn the concept of sorting—in this case, big and little lambs.*

**Words to use**

big
little
sort

**Materials**

two sizes of cutout lambs—big and little
two boxes or baskets

**What to do**

1. Help the children sort the lambs according to size.
2. Use one box or basket for the small lambs and the other for the big lambs.

★ WHERE IS THUMBKIN?

# Whose Hat Is This?

**3+**

*Children learn about their community and the people who work in it.*

**Words to use**

hats
wear
match
jobs
work
community
help
cook
teacher
crosswalk guard
janitor

### Materials

pictures of hats and people who wear them
plastic container

### What to do

1. Collect pictures of hats and the people who wear them.
2. Place them in a plastic container.
3. The children match and identify a hat for each wearer.
4. Pictures of people who work in the school, wearing their hats, make the activity more meaningful. Examples include cooks, janitor, nurse, crosswalk guard or public safety officer.

★ THE COMPLETE LEARNING CENTER BOOK

# Key Match

### 3+

*Children learn visual discrimination skills.*

### Words to use

match
shape
color
key

### Materials

keys
tagboard or poster
board
marker

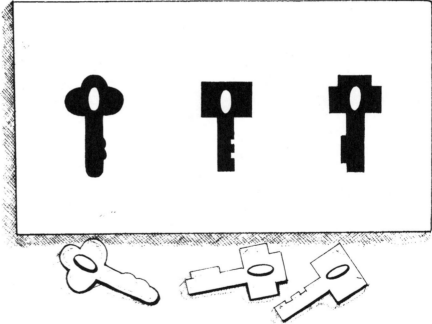

### What to do

1. Place the keys on the poster board and trace around each one. Color the keys if you like.
2. Ask the children to match the keys to the shapes on the poster board.

★ WHERE IS THUMBKIN?

# Tea Cup Match

**3+**

*Children learn one-to-one correspondence.*

## Words to use

tea
cup
saucer
match

## Materials

tea cups and saucers

## What to do

Ask the children to match the cups with the correct saucers.

★ WHERE IS THUMBKIN?

# Muffin Patterns

**3+**

*Children learn patterning skills.*

## Words to use

cupcake
muffin
color words
pattern

## Materials

paper cupcake/muffin holders of at least two different colors
muffin tin

## What to do

1. The children create a pattern in the muffin tin using the different colors of cupcake/muffin holders.
2. Ask the older children to create a pattern for the younger children to follow.

★ WHERE IS THUMBKIN?

# Twig Race

**3+**

*The Twig Race utilizes observation of the marvel of spring—the renewed growth of trees as buds and leaves grow from their twigs. But which grows fastest, the twig on the tree or the cut twig that is taken inside? Children observe the growth of the twigs both indoors and out. Who wins the race? Try it and find out!*

## Words to use

| | |
|---|---|
| twig | leaves |
| emerge | bud |
| spring | bud scars |
| observe | window |
| sunlight | roots |
| compare | |

## Materials

a tree
a twig from this tree
yarn
clippers
knife
jar

## What to do

1. Very early in spring, before the buds on trees begin to swell, take the children outside to look at a tree. Talk about the lack of leaves and explain that they will begin to grow as the weather gets warmer and the days get longer. Carefully cut a small twig from the tree so that the children can observe it more closely. Talk about the bud. Is it furry, smooth, shiny? What color is it?
2. Tell the children that leaves will grow on a twig that is cut off the tree if it is taken care of properly. Let's see which twig sprouts first, the one the tree takes care of, or the one we take care of. Tie a piece of brightly colored yarn on the twig which you wish to observe outdoors so that you can always find the same one. Take the cut twig inside. Place it in a jar of water by a window.
3. Observe the two twigs until leaves form. Which twig wins the race?

## Want to do more?

Continue to observe the twigs. Some twigs will sprout roots, others will die. Compare the twigs of pussy willow, forsythia or flowering trees. Compare them with and without water and with and without light. Compare different types of trees. Which loses its leaves first? Last? In the fall when the leaves drop, count how many are left on the twig.

★ MUDPIES TO MAGNETS

# Measure Shadows

*Shadows come in all shapes and sizes. Even a single object produces a shadow that varies with the time of day and the seasons. In this activity children can observe and record changes in shadows from season to season.*

## Words to use

winter
spring
summer
fall
seasons
big
bigger
small
smaller
size
shadow

## Materials

permanent objects in the yard or on the playground, i.e., garbage can, swing set, clothesline pole, climbing frame, flag pole, tree, bush

stakes with ribbons colored differently for each season

## What to do

1. Inside or outside, discuss shadows.
2. Make some with your hands and with your bodies.
3. Go outside and look for shadows. Discuss how large the shadow is.
4. Measure it and mark it with the colored stakes.
5. Repeat the activity at different times of the day. Are the shadows longer or shorter? Why?
6. Repeat the activity as the seasons pass.
7. Photograph at least one shadow each season. Do the shadows remain the same size? Are they different? Why?

## Want to do more?

Repeat the above procedure, only this time use chalk and trace around the shadows. Do this at various times of the day and during different seasons. Compare your various tracings. Using a strong flashlight, make a shadow of your hand on the wall. Next, use items from outside— pine cones, branches, plants—and let the children identify what the shadows are.

★ Hug a Tree

# Music and Movement Activities

## Let's Be the Wind

**3+**

*Children use creative movement to learn about wind.*

### Words to use

feel          sound
blow          wind
weather

### Materials

crepe paper streamers, two to three feet long, one per child
"Who Has Seen the Wind" by Christina Rosetti, or another poem or fingerplay about wind

### What to do

1. Gather the children into a sitting group. Read a book about wind to the children or recite a poem (or the poem mentioned above) or do a fingerplay.
2. Review or discuss what the children know about wind. Ask questions: Can you hear wind? Can you make a sound like wind? Can you feel the wind? How does it feel against your body? Can someone show us how you would walk if the wind were blowing hard? What kind of weather can we have when the wind is blowing?
3. Tell children they will pretend they are the wind. Allow enough space for children to move while twirling streamers. Define your space boundaries and give each child a streamer.
4. Have them wave the streamers around in front of them, to the side, over their heads.
5. Encourage the children to move as if they were the wind. Guide them with words: "Blow high in the air, blow down to the ground, twirl around and around. Be a strong wind, be a gentle wind, settle down, down, down to the ground."
6. After moving for a while, sit down again. Ask the children what they liked best about pretending to be the wind.

### Want to do more?

Ask children to pretend they are kites flying on a windy day. Make or buy a wind sock to observe wind direction outdoors.

### Book to read

*The Wind Blew* by Pat Hutchins

★ THE GIANT ENCYCLOPEDIA OF THEME ACTIVITIES

# Walk Like a Lamb

*Children use their large muscles in this activity.*

**Words to use**

crawl
lamb
act out

**Materials**

recording of "Mary Had a Little Lamb"

**What to do**

1. Play the music and ask the children to crawl on all fours to imitate Mary's lamb.
2. Act out the story in the song.

★ Where Is Thumbkin?


# Walking the Bridge

**3+**

*This activity develops coordination.*

**Words to use**

bridge
cross
beanbag

**Materials**

masking tape
beanbag

**What to do**

1. Place two or three 6-foot strips of masking tape on the floor.
2. Encourage the children to walk the masking tape line (bridge).
3. Challenge the children to cross the "bridge" with a beanbag on their heads.

★ Where Is Thumbkin?

# Magic Wand

**3+**

*This activity reinforces children's positional vocabulary.*

## Words to use

position
over
under
between
beside

## Materials

scarves
recorded music

## What to do

1. Provide each child with a scarf to use as a "magic wand."
2. Begin playing a record.
3. Direct children to wave their "magic wand" *over* their head, *under* the table, *between* their legs, *beside* a chair, and so on.

★ The Instant Curriculum

# Around the Chairs

**3+**

*This activity encourages the development of large motor skills.*

## Words to use

move
walk
tiptoe
hop
skate
gallop

## Materials

chairs
recorded music

## What to do

1. Place a line of chairs in the center of the room to make a traffic island.
2. Put a record on and have children go around the chairs in different ways: walk, tiptoe, hop, skate, gallop, skip.

★ The Instant Curriculum

# Guess the Song

3+

*This activity teaches children body awareness.*

## Words to use

melody
rhythm
hum
snap
stamp

## Materials

## What to do

1. Pick a popular song that the children enjoy singing, like "Twinkle, Twinkle, Little Star."
2. Sing the song together.
3. Show the children how to "sing" using another part of the body to carry the melody or rhythm, for example: hum, click tongue, clap hands, snap fingers, stamp feet.
4. Try singing the song one of these ways.
5. Clap out the rhythm of another familiar song, and see whether the children can identify it.

★ 500 FIVE MINUTE GAMES

# A Sailor Went to Sea

3+

*Use this song to let children stretch and wiggle and quiet themselves down. Children have fun doing the motions as they sing the nonsense words.*

## Words to use

sing
sail
sailor
sea
see

## Materials

## What to do

1. Stand up straight like sailors, then begin singing.

> A sailor went to sea, sea, sea. (put hand over eye as if saluting)
> To see what he could see, see, see.
> And all that he could see, see, see,
> Was the bottom of the deep blue sea, sea, sea.
>
> A sailor went to chop, chop, chop. (make chopping motion with arm)
> To see what he could chop, chop, chop.
> And all that he could chop, chop, chop,
> Was the bottom of the deep blue chop, chop, chop.
>
> A sailor went to knee, knee, knee.... (touch knee)
> A sailor went to tap, tap, tap.... (tap toe)
> A sailor went to washy-wash.... (put hands on hips and wiggle)

2. For the last verse, put all the motions together.

> A sailor went to sea, chop, knee, tap, washy-wash.
> To see what he could see, chop, knee, tap, washy-wash.
> And all that he could see, chop, knee, tap, washy-wash,
> Was the bottom of the deep blue sea, chop, knee, tap, washy-wash.

★ TRANSITION TIME

# Science Activities

## Frozen Nature Collages

**3+**

*Children notice how the temperature affects water.*

### Words to use

| | |
|---|---|
| freeze | frozen |
| melt | sheltered |
| watch | observe |
| sunlight | cold |
| warm | warmth |

### Materials

disposable pie tins
materials from nature such as pine needles, pine cones, twigs or acorns
water
food coloring, optional
yarn and scissors
masking tape and marker
freezing weather or a freezer

### What to do

1. Fill the pie tins with water. Let the children place various objects from nature in their tin.
2. Put in a drop or two of food coloring if you wish (let the children choose their colors).
3. Place the ends of a loop of yarn in the water. This will be used as a hanger later.
4. Print each child's name on a piece of masking tape and attach it to the yarn.
5. Place the tins in a sheltered spot outside and allow them to freeze solid. It's nice if you place them near a window where the children can watch them from inside the classroom. Or you can freeze them in a freezer.
6. When they are solidly frozen, pour some warm water on the back of the pie tins to unmold the ice. Then hang these beautiful things from a tree or the fence so the sunlight can shine through to decorate the playground.
7. Over time, the children can watch what happens to their ice collages as the weather gets warmer.

★ THE OUTSIDE PLAY AND LEARNING BOOK

# Round Wind Wands

**3+**

*These Wind Wands or Round Wind Catchers make a fun and lovely activity for those first warm spring days.*

## Words to use

| | |
|---|---|
| streamers | wand |
| catch the wind | round |
| circle | wind |
| blow | run |

## Materials

cane—one piece per child, approximately 36" long

masking tape

streamers—the crepe paper variety, approximately 1 to 1-1/4" wide and 18-24" long, in springtime colors

transparent tape

## What to do

1. Start with a piece of cane about 36 inches long. If the cane is thin, make it more sturdy by holding both ends together and twisting it so that it wraps around itself.
2. Now bend the (twisted) cane into a round shape and thoroughly secure the ends with masking tape. You want to have a circle that is at least 5 inches in diameter.
3. Have the children select five to seven streamers.
4. Attach the streamers side by side by folding a streamer end over the cane and taping it both to itself and to the caning.
5. Take the wind wands outside and "catch" the wind with them. Some children may want to run with the wind to catch even more wind.

Note: These round wands are good for younger children because they can't poke anyone accidentally.

★ EARTHWAYS

# Wind-o-Meter

*Children experience the wind by holding up a wind-o-meter.*

## Words to use

wind
blow
direction

## Materials

one strip of wind cloth (Aspen cloth, Rip-stop, taffeta-type cloth), 2" x 45"

## What to do

1. Assemble children outside and have them hold the cloth (wind-o-meter) with outstretched arms.
2. Have children observe which way the wind-o-meter is blowing and deduce which way the wind is blowing.
3. Have the children run into the wind to see what happens to the wind-o-meter (it really flies).
4. Have the children run with the wind to see what happens to the wind-o-meter (it may stop flying altogether).
5. Have the children run at right angles to the wind and observe their wind-o-meter.

## Want to do more?

Use the wind-o-meter in the gym or classroom where children create all the wind. Fasten several wind-o-meters together and observe and state what happens to a longer wind-o-meter.

★ THE GIANT ENCYCLOPEDIA OF THEME ACTIVITIES

# Streamers

3+

*Moving air is called wind. Wind makes things move. What happens when the wind doesn't blow? Can we make our own wind? How? This activity shows how we can do the work of the wind ourselves.*

## Words to use

| | |
|---|---|
| wind | blow |
| flow | run |
| fast | slow |
| work | direction |

## Materials

paper streamers
straws
stapler
fan

## What to do

1. Attach 4 paper streamers to each straw. Use a stapler to attach.
2. Have children hold the streamers in front of a fan. Observe how the wind blows them.
3. Go outside. Does the wind blow the streamers? What happens when the wind doesn't blow?
4. Let's run with our streamers.
5. What happens to the streamers when we run? Can you run fast enough to make your streamers fly straight behind?
6. How did we do the work of the wind?

## Want to do more?

Follow a direction game. "Make circles with your streamers. Make your streamers wiggle. Make your streamers flow in circles around your arm." Have a streamer parade for a special occasion. Make materials available so children can make their own using the colors of your school or a favorite sports team. What can you do to keep your streamers from flying out behind you when you run?

★ MORE MUDPIES TO MAGNETS

# Jumping on Air                                          3+

*This activity demonstrates in an active, participatory and fun way that air takes up space and, in fact, does work for us. When the children have caught the air, they can have the air catch them.*

## Words to use

air
strong
fall
blow
tie
compressed air
jump
secure
pump

## Materials

plastic produce bags from the grocery store
plastic-type ties
large garbage bags

fill large trash bag with smaller plastic produce bags filled with air and sealed.

## What to do

1. Blow up a plastic bag. Secure it with a tie. Let a child sit on it. What happens? It will pop, or the air will eventually leak out.
2. Discuss the fact that one bag is not strong enough to hold us up. How can we make it stronger? By adding more bags and bunching them together we can create a cushion of air that can support not only one child but many.
3. Let the children help blow up numerous plastic produce bags from the grocery store. Use tie tops to secure tightly.
4. Place many inflated bags into a large garbage bag. Secure the bag with a tie when it is stuffed with the air filled produce bags.
5. Let the children one at a time sit on, fall onto, or jump into the bags if you have 4 or 5 large bags.
6. What happens? Did the bags burst? Why not? The air distributed and formed a natural cushion for the children as they jumped. It's as strong as air.

★ MORE MUDPIES TO MAGNETS

# Move That Air!                                    3+

*This activity teaches children about vibrations.*

## Words to use

vibrate
vibration
hum
vocal cords

## Materials

## What to do

1. Explain to the children that sound is made when air moves. The movement is called vibration.
2. Ask the children to touch their hands to their throats and hum. Feel the vibration.
3. Explain to the children that their throats contain vocal cords that move back and forth when they talk.
4. When they hum, they can feel the vocal cords moving back and forth.
5. Hold the palm of one hand in front of your face. Blow on the palm.
6. While blowing, move the index finger of your other hand through the air flow. Listen to the sound change.

★ 500 FIVE MINUTE GAMES

# Falling Down
**3+**

*This simple activity teaches observation skills.*

### Words to use

fall down          drop
fast               slowly

### Materials

tissue
feather
jar lid
block
leaves
baskets

### What to do

1. Talk about things that fall down, for example, rain, children, snow, leaves, etc.
2. Let the children drop various items into the baskets and observe which ones fall fast and which ones fall slowly.

★ WHERE IS THUMBKIN?

# Make Your Own Greenhouse
**3+**

*A greenhouse is designed to trap sunlight, heat and water. The clear surface of the skin of the greenhouse allows light to pass through and warm the inside air, keeping the plants in tropical conditions year round. When adequate water is available, the high humidity adds to the factors that influence even faster and more luxuriant growth. You can create a large greenhouse to simulate an actual building by using plastic over a wooden frame, or you can use our mini-greenhouse set up.*

### Words to use

sunlight
humidity
growth
greenhouse
estimate

### Materials

clear plastic cup
potting soil
water
grass seed
cake pan

## What to do

1. Plant grass seed in a cake pan.
2. Water lightly. A spray bottle works well.
3. Place a clear plastic cup over a section of the tray. Place in sunlight.
4. Water lightly as needed.
5. Observe the growth.
6. Let the children estimate the height that they feel the grass in the greenhouse (plastic cup) will be after five days.
7. Estimate the growth of the non-greenhouse grass.
8. Which do you think will grow fastest and highest?
9. Each time you measure the grass, ask the children to estimate how much more it will grow in another given time period.

## Want to do more?

Visit the local nursery. Let the children see the plants. Talk with the owner about the plants and how they are cared for in a greenhouse. Plant other seeds in your greenhouse. Can the children figure out a way to make a bigger greenhouse? Let them try out their ideas, even those you don't think will work. They will learn from the process whether it works or not.

★ MORE MUDPIES TO MAGNETS

# Adopt a Tree                                    3+

*This activity asks children to become involved with life outside their classroom, life over which they have little control. They begin here to expand the radius of their responsibility.*

## Words to use

life
growing up
gentle
care
responsibility
healthy

## Materials

fertilizers
water buckets
simple gardening tools

## What to do

1. Tell the children that they are going to find a little tree outside for the class to "adopt." This means that everyone will have some responsibility for keeping the tree healthy so that it will grow up big and strong.
2. Take the children outside and look for the youngest tree within easy walking distance of your school.

3. Sit around the tree and discuss what it needs to be healthy. What kind of care does the tree need from the children? How will this care change over the rest of the school year? Identify the specific caretaking actions the children will do: pulling weeds, trimming grass, fertilizing, providing water from buckets, mulching around the base of the trunk and checking for harmful bugs.
4. During the next week, assign responsibilities for taking care of the tree and form a plan for continued care for the rest of the year.
5. Revisit the tree occasionally to check its progress.

### Want to do more?

Invite a horticulturist to visit your group to talk about caring for trees. Conduct a field trip to a lawn and garden store.

### Book to read

*A Mother for Choco* by Keiko Kasza

### Home connection

Parents and children can visit a local park and adopt a young tree growing in a primitive area that receives no maintenance from park personnel. They can take care of the tree during periodic visits. A picnic near the tree may be nice at certain times of the year.

★ THE PEACEFUL CLASSROOM

# Can You Tell by Looking?                    4+

*This activity encourages the development of observation skills.*

### Words to use

look                    examine
identify                magnify

### Materials

salt
sugar
flour
baking soda
wax paper
magnifying glass

### What to do

1. Place a small amount of sugar, salt, flour and baking soda on separate pieces of wax paper.
2. The children look at the four substances and try to identify what they are.
3. Look again using a magnifying glass.
4. Invite the children to taste a small amount of each as a final check.

★ WHERE IS THUMBKIN?

# Pinwheels

**4+**

*Pinwheels are fun on a breezy day. See what the wind can do, or children can create a wind of their own by running or blowing.*

## Words to use

breezy
blow
turn
spin
pinwheel

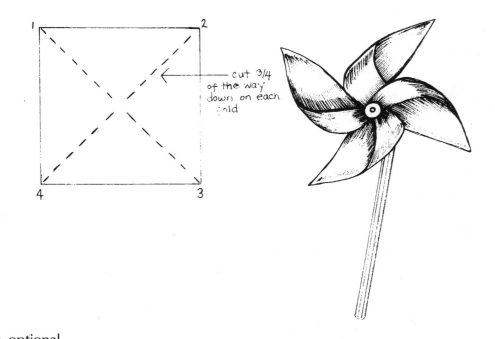

cut 3/4 of the way down on each fold

## Materials

colored construction paper or heavy white watercolor paper that the children decorate with crayons
scissors
straight pins
new, unsharpened pencils with erasers
scissors
scraps of paper and tape, optional

## What to do

1. Cut the paper into 7-inch squares. You can vary the size with a larger square, but the pinwheel will be more floppy. Don't make it bigger than 8-1/2 inches.
2. Determine the center of the square (see illustration). This is done by lightly folding tip number one to tip number three and tip number four to tip number two. You don't need a strong crease. The center is where the two folds intersect.
3. Now, using the scissors, cut in on each fold line about 3/4 of the way to the center. Leave the last inch of each fold uncut.
4. With a pin and pencil ready, fold every other tip (you now have eight) into the center and overlap them. Push the pin through these overlapping tips, through the center of the pinwheel and into the eraser. Don't let the pin stick out the other side of the eraser.
Note: A little paper washer reinforces the center of the pinwheel. Cut a small circle of colored paper (about 1 to 1-1/2 inches in diameter). This doesn't have to be a perfect circle—just do it freehand. Put a tape loop on the back of the circle and press it onto the overlapping tips of paper at the pinwheel's center. Then insert the pin. This provides extra support at the stress point.
5. Show the children how to make the pinwheel turn by blowing on it. Then let them take the pinwheels outdoors and see what the wind can do.

★ EARTHWAYS

# Air Resistance Race

**4+**

*The race we are proposing is one designed to show that air resistance is present and is a factor even in such a simple thing as a running race. See you on the starting line.*

## Words to use

wind
resistance
race
relay
time
timer
clock
run
compare
aerodynamic

## Materials

timer
3' by 3' piece of tagboard or cardboard (scale the size of cardboard down or up to fit size of your children)

## What to do

1. Have the children line up single file. Designate a starting and an ending point.
2. On a signal, the first child runs to the marker and returns to tag the next child in the line. This procedure continues until all have run the course. The entire run is timed with a kitchen timer. How many minutes did it take for the entire class to run the relay? Record it.
3. Now repeat the entire process, only this time the runners must hold the 3' x 3' cardboard piece in front of them. Be sure the cardboard doesn't block the runner's vision.
4. Compare the times. Did the air pushing on the cardboard slow you down? Was there more air resistance with the cardboard or without it? Why?

## Want to do more?

Repeat this procedure with larger pieces of cardboard. Try this on a windy day. Run against the wind, then with the wind.

★ MORE MUDPIES TO MAGNETS

# Balloon Fliers

*When we blow up a balloon and let it go, the air is discharged in one direction and produces a thrust that moves the balloon rapidly about the room. Other forces, gravity and friction, act to slow the balloon down. The long string will cause the balloon to slow down faster, but it provides a necessary tool to compare the amount of force released by the air escaping from each balloon.*

## Words to use

rockets
balloons
air
force
thrust
far
farthest
more
most
gravity

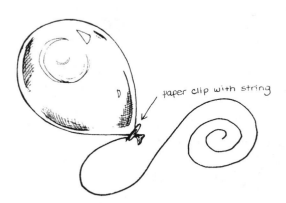

paper clip with string

## Materials

balloons
paper clips
very light string cut in 15 ft. lengths

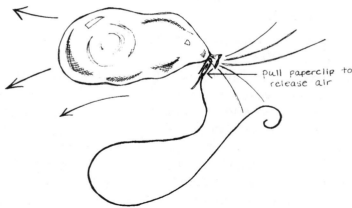

pull paperclip to release air

## What to do

1. Tie one end of a 15 ft. coil of string to a paper clip. Blow up the balloon and hold the opening tight. Clip the string to the balloon.
2. Let the children take turns letting their balloons blast off.
3. Where did it land? How far did it go? Compare distances by comparing the amount of string each one used. Make a graph. Why do some balloons travel farther than others?

## Want to do more?

Use 3 different sized balloons. Which size balloon travels farthest?

★ MORE MUDPIES TO MAGNETS

# To Move or Not to Move

*Children compare the effects of air movement on objects of varying weights, and they learn to use graphs.*

## Words to use

graph
sort
heavy
light

## Materials

four egg cartons with tops
    removed
markers
four lunch bags or small plastic
    containers
variety of small objects of varying
    weights
drinking straw for each child

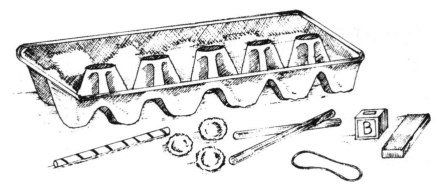

## What to do

1. After removing the tops from each egg carton, decorate one row of each carton with a smile and the word yes.
2. Decorate the other side of each carton with a frown and the word no. The cartons will be used as a graph during the activity.
3. Collect a variety of objects that vary in weight—cotton balls, popsicle sticks, small plastic blocks, small wooden blocks, plastic animals, paper, paper clips, sea shells and rubber bands.
4. Place eight to ten different objects in each lunch bag or plastic container.
5. Color each bag or container so they can be distinguished from one another.
6. Place materials, egg carton graphs and containers of objects in the science center.
7. Have each child choose one plastic container and an egg carton graph.
8. The child should then experiment with the objects in the container to determine which objects can be moved when blown with the straw and which ones cannot.
9. The child should place the objects on the correct side of the graph, one object per cup in the carton.
10. The children may experiment with all containers of objects.
11. Encourage discussions among the children in the center. Have them compare among themselves which objects seemed to be heavier, which seemed to be lighter, as well as why some objects would move and others would not.

## Want to do more?

Have the children make and record predictions. The children can then refer back to the chart to check the predictions as each object is tested. The actual results of the experiment could then be recorded on a wall graph for later reference. A fan may also be used to provide air movement.

★ THE GIANT ENCYCLOPEDIA OF THEME ACTIVITIES

# Snack and Cooking Activities

## Breakfast Muffins

3+

*Children taste a variety of breakfast muffins.*

### Words to use

taste
surprise
pick
select
snack

### Materials

a variety of wheat muffins, bran muffins, banana-nut muffins, any of the fruit muffins recommended for breakfast
baskets or serving dishes
colorful napkins
apple juice

### What to do

1. The best activity would be to bake the muffins with the children helping you. However, if this isn't possible, another good beginning is to involve some of the children in helping you select the muffins at the bakery. If neither step is possible, choose a wide variety of breakfast muffins and bring them to class.
2. Have several children help you arrange them on serving dishes or in baskets. Cover the snack surprises with colorful napkins.
3. Tell the children what kinds of muffins you have brought them, and tell them where you purchased them.
4. Have them select their muffin and pour their own apple juice.

### Teaching tips

Large muffins may need to be cut in half for young children. When they choose the fruit muffins, talk about whether they like the fresh fruit or the muffins better. Warm the muffins in a microwave for more appealing taste and aroma.

★ STORY S-T-R-E-T-C-H-E-R-S

# Blueberry Muffins

3+

*Children learn to read a rebus recipe for making blueberry muffins.*

**Words to use**

rebus
picture
read

**Materials**

chart tablet or poster board and marker
blueberry muffin mix
egg
water
mixing bowl and wooden spoon
measuring cup
muffin tin
oven mitt
toaster oven
bread baskets
napkins
cartons of milk
glasses

**What to do**

1. Print the recipe for blueberry muffins on a chart tablet or poster board. Use a combination of symbols and words. For example, when the next step is mixing the ingredients, draw a mixing bowl and spoon. (See the page 257 for a sample rebus symbol chart.)
2. Divide the class into two groups, as it will probably take two packages of the mix to make enough muffins for everyone.
3. Assign some children to measure, others to mix and some to serve the muffins. Mix and cook the muffins.
4. Place napkins in bread baskets. Empty the muffins into the bread baskets and place on the snack table.
5. Serve the muffins warm with a cold glass or carton of milk.

**Teaching tips**

If possible, ask a parent or community volunteer to come to the classroom and make the muffins from scratch.

~Making Blueberry Muffins~

1. Preheat
2. Place ▢ in
3. Empty Mix into
4. Add ◯ and ½ ☕ water
5. Stir
6. Pour into
7. Bake in
8. Serve and

★ MORE STORY S-T-R-E-T-C-H-E-R-S

# Cheese and Crackers                                        3+

*Children learn to use a cheese slicer.*

## Words to use

slice
cheese
prefer
like best
demonstrate
show
sample
serve

## Materials

variety of mild cheeses in rounds and blocks
cheese slicer
crackers
pitcher
juice
plates
napkins

## What to do

1. Demonstrate how to use a cheese slicer.
2. Tell the children about the names of the cheeses you have selected.
3. Let the children slice samples of the different cheeses. Serve with the crackers and their favorite juice.
4. During snack time, ask the children to tell which cheese they prefer.

## Teaching tips

Also consider serving cheese logs and a cheese spread. Let the children cut and spread the cheese preparations. If your state has a cheese product, be sure to serve a local cheese as well.

★ MORE STORY S-T-R-E-T-C-H-E-R-S

snack & cooking activities

 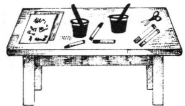

# Transition Activities

## Take Home Kits

**3+**

*Encourage children and parents to check these out and take them home at the end of the day. Besides building a home/school partnership, the activities in these kits suggest other materials parents can give their children to play with at home.*

### Words to use

kit
learning
take home
parents
directions

### Materials

detergent boxes with handles
spray paint

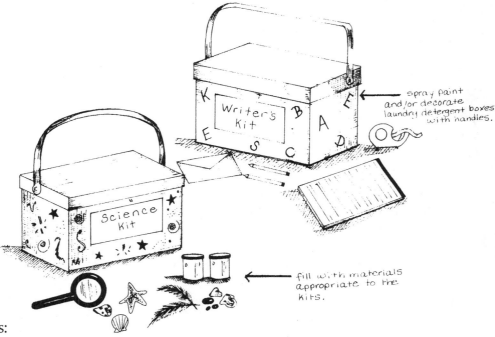

*spray paint and/or decorate laundry detergent boxes with handles.*

*fill with materials appropriate to the kits.*

### What to do

1. Spray paint the boxes, or let the children decorate them.
2. Fill the boxes with the following kits or materials:
   ✓ writer's kit—blank paper, envelopes, pens, pencils, tape, etc.
   ✓ math kit—ruler, dice, set cards, shape stencils, paper and pencils, play money, etc.
   ✓ art kit—scissors, markers, crayons, paper, glue, paper sacks, paper plates, collage materials, etc.
   ✓ science kit—magnifying glass, magnet, collections of shells, rocks, seeds, etc.
   ✓ blank books and markers
   ✓ sewing cards
   ✓ playdough and cookie cutters
   ✓ puppets or little toys, books, children's magazines
   ✓ scrap paper and hole punch
   ✓ homemade puzzles (cut up the front of cardboard food boxes into puzzle shapes)
   ✓ homemade card games and matching games
3. Put the directions in the box.
4. Let the children choose a different one to take home every night or week.

★ TRANSITION TIME

# Buddy Bunny

*Buddy Bunny chooses a different child to go home with every day. Language skills and parental involvement are enhanced with this take-home story.*

## Words to use

backpack
bunny
rabbit
mischief
notebook
story
write
dictate
imagine
imagination
circle time

## Materials

stuffed animal (bunny, bear, etc.)
cloth bag or backpack
spiral ring notebook

## What to do

1. Put the bunny (or other animal) in the backpack or bag, along with the notebook.
2. Write a note to go in the bag similar to the following one.

> *Dear Parents,*
>
> *Today your child is bringing home Buddy Bunny. Buddy loves children and he loves to get into mischief. Please write a story in the notebook about what Buddy does with your child. You may want to let your child dictate a story for you to write. We'll read the story tomorrow at school.*
>
> *Thank you! Have fun!*

3. Choose a different child each day to take Buddy Bunny and the bag home.
4. Read what the parents have written the next morning at circle time.

## Want to do more?

Add a book, toothbrush, change of clothes or other props to go along with Buddy Bunny. Older children can write their own adventures with Buddy Bunny.

★ TRANSITION TIME

# Note Tote

**3+**

*Fill the Note Tote with children's paintings, letters to parents and other papers at the end of the day. Sometimes children drop their papers. This will be a handy way to keep things together.*

## Words to use

cardboard
roll
round
tube
tote
carry
decorate
papers
notes
parents
home
mail
deliver

## Materials

cardboard rollers (paper towel rolls)
markers
crayons
stickers
collage materials and glue

## What to do

1. Give each child a cardboard roller. Write her name on it.
2. Let the children decorate their rollers with markers, crayons, stickers, magazine pictures or other collage materials.
3. Before the children go home, tell them to get their papers, roll them up and put them in their Note Tote.
4. Have them pretend they are mail carriers and deliver their notes and pictures to their parents.

## Want to do more?

Give children large grocery sacks to decorate to take their work home in. Let children decorate detergent boxes with handles to use to take home papers.

★ TRANSITION TIME

# The March Wind                                            3+

*This activity encourages children's creativity.*

## Words to use

blow
wind
tree
rush

## Materials

## What to do

1. Play a March Wind game.
2. The children form a circle and pretend that they are trees.
3. Each child can be a different kind of tree. Ask the children what kind of tree they are.
4. Choose one child to be the wind.
5. The wind rushes in and out of the trees making a sound like blowing wind.
6. The trees bend back and forth in the blowing wind.
7. At a signal, the wind stops and trades places with a tree.
8. One child who was a tree becomes the wind, and the game continues.

★ 500 FIVE MINUTE GAMES

# Margery Daw                                               3+

*This activity helps children develop social skills.*

## Words to use

partner
hands
rock
back and forth
seesaw

### Materials

### What to do

1. Seat the children on the floor, facing a partner.
2. Partners hold hands, rocking back and forth on an imaginary seesaw. Recite the following nursery rhyme as they rock.

> *Seesaw, Margery Daw,*
> *Jackie shall have a new master.*
> *He shall have but a penny a day,*
> *Because he can't work any faster.*
> *(repeat)*

★ 500 FIVE MINUTE GAMES

# Nursery Rhyme Game 3+

*This activity encourages the development of memory and language skills.*

### Words to use

clue
identify
nursery rhymes
song
materials
book of nursery rhymes, optional

### Materials

### What to do

1. Quote lines from favorite nursery rhymes or songs.
2. Ask the children to identify the people in the rhymes.
3. For example, "Two people I know went up the hill to fetch a pail of water."
4. The children will answer "Jack and Jill."
5. Here are some other ideas.

> *Someone had a little lamb, little lamb, little lamb*
> *Someone is nimble, he is also quick*
> *Someone had a farm, E-I-E-I-O*

★ 500 FIVE MINUTE GAMES

# The Little Toad

*An enjoyable way to develop children's coordination.*

**Words to use**

hop
sleep
peep
catch
wink

**Materials**

**What to do**

Recite the poem and perform the actions.

> *I am a little toad,*
> *Hopping down the road. (hop fingers)*
> *Just listen to my song,*
> *I sleep all winter long. (pretend to be sleeping)*
> *When spring comes, I peep out,*
> *And then I jump about. (move arms around)*
> *And now I catch a fly, (pretend to catch something)*
> *And now I wink my eye, (wink one eye)*
> *And now and then I hop, (hop around)*
> *And now and then I stop. (stop hopping)*

★ 500 FIVE MINUTE GAMES

# Books

*Aunt Flossie's Hats (and Crab Cakes Later)* by Elizabeth Howard
*Caps for Sale* by Esphyr Slobodkina
*Egg to Chick* by Millicent Selsam
*First Comes Spring* by Anne Rockwell
*Gilberto and the Wind* by Marie Hall Ets
*Ho for a Hat!* by William J. Smith
*Home in the Sky* by Jeannie Baker
*Horton Hatches an Egg* by Dr. Seuss
*Jennie's Hat* by Ezra Jack Keats
*The Listening Walk* by Paul Showers
*Martin's Hats* by Joan W. Blos
*Mary Had a Little Lamb* by Sarah J. Hale
*Miss Rumphius* by Barbara Cooney
*Mud Puddle* by Robert N. Munsch
*My Spring Robin* by Anne Rockwell
*Over the Moon* by Charlotte Voake
*Pelle's New Suit* by Elsa Beskow
*The Random House Book of Mother Goose: A Treasury of 306 Timeless Nursery Rhymes*
*Sheep in a Jeep* by Nancy Shaw
*The Story of the Root Children* by Sibylle von Olfers
*The Sun's Asleep behind the Hill* by Mirra Ginsburg
*That's What Happens When It's Spring!* by Elaine Good
*This Year's Garden* by Cynthia Rylant
*The Three Billy Goats Gruff* by Ellen Appleby
A *Tree Is Nice* by Janice May Udry
*Wendy Watson's Mother Goose* by Wendy Watson
*Will Spring Be Early? Or Will Spring Be Late?* by Crockett Johnson
*The Wind Blew* by Pat Hutchins

# Records, Tapes and CDs

Beall, Pamela Conn and Susan Hagen Nipp. "Jack and Jill" from *Wee Sing Nursery Rhymes and Lullabies*. Price Stern Sloan. 1985.

Sharon, Lois and Bram. "Jack and Jill" from *Mainly Mother Goose*. Elephant, 1984.

Beall, Pamela Conn and Susan Hagen Nipp. "Mary Had a Little Lamb" from *Wee Sing Nursery Rhymes and Lullabies*. Price Stern Sloan, 1985.

Buck, Dennis. "Mary Had a Little Lamb" from *Singable Nursery Rhymes*. Kimbo, 1986.

Scelsa, Greg and Steve Millang. "Muffin Man" from *We All Live Together*, Volume 2, Youngheart Records.

Sharon, Lois and Bram. "Muffin Man" from *Singing 'n Swinging*. Elephant Records, 1980.

# Spring

# Fingerplays, Poems and Songs

## Doctor Foster

Doctor Foster went to Glo'ster
In a shower of rain;
He stepped in a puddle
Up to his middle
And never went there again.

★ ONE POTATO, TWO POTATO, THREE POTATO, FOUR

## One Misty, Moisty Morning

One misty, moisty morning
When cloudy was the weather,
I met a little old man
Clothed all in leather.

Clothed all in leather,
With a strap under his chin.
And he said, "How do you do?"
And "How do you do?"
And "How do you do?" again.

★ ONE POTATO, TWO POTATO, THREE POTATO, FOUR

## Five Little Birdies

Five little birds, sitting on my door.
One jumped off, then there were four.
Four little birdies happy as can be.
One flew away, and then there were three.
Three little birds with nothing to do.
One fell off, then there were two.
Two little birds chirping in the sun.
A bird flew away, then there was one.
One little bird sitting in the sun.
Away he flew, and there were none.

★ TRANSITION TIME

## It's Raining, It's Pouring

It's raining, it's pouring,
The old man is snoring.
He went to bed with a pain in his head
And didn't get up until morning.

★ ONE POTATO, TWO POTATO, THREE POTATO, FOUR

## Rain on the Green Grass

Rain on the green grass
And rain on the tree;
Rain on the housetop
But not on me.

★ ONE POTATO, TWO POTATO, THREE POTATO, FOUR

## Mistress Mary, Quite Contrary

Mistress Mary, quite contrary
How does your garden grow?
With silver bells and cockle shells
And pretty maids all in a row.

## Over in the Meadow

Over in the meadow, in the sand, in the sun,
Lived an old mother frog and her little froggie
   one.
"Croak!" said the mother, "I croak," said the
   one,
So they croaked and they croaked in the sand,
   in the sun.

Over in the meadow, in the stream so blue,
Lived an old mother fish and her little fishies two.
"Swim!" said the mother, "We swim!" said the
    two,
So they swam and they swam in the stream so
    blue.

Over in the meadow, on a branch of the tree,
Lived an old mother bird and her little birdies
    three.
"Sing!" said the mother, "We sing!" said the
    three,
So they sang and they sang on a branch of the
    tree.

★ WHERE IS THUMBKIN?

# Eensy Weensy Spider

The eensy weensy spider
Climbed up the water spout.
Down came the rain
And washed the spider out.

Out came the sun
And dried up all the rain,
And the eensy weensy spider
Climbed up the spout again.

★ WHERE IS THUMBKIN?

# Rain, Rain

Rain, rain, go away,
Come again another day;
Rain, rain, go away,
Little (Johnny) wants to play.

★ WHERE IS THUMBKIN?

# One Elephant

One elephant went out to play,
Out on a spider's web one day,
He had such enormous fun,
He called for another elephant to come.

★ WHERE IS THUMBKIN?

# The Green Grass Grows All Around

There was a tree. (echo)
All in the wood. (echo)
The prettiest little tree. (echo)
That you ever did see. (echo)
The tree in a hole, and the hole in the ground
And the green grass grew all around, all around,
And the green grass grew all around.

And on that tree. (echo)
There was a limb. (echo)
The prettiest little limb. (echo)
That you ever did see. (echo)
The limb on the tree, and the tree in a hole,
And the green grass grew all around, all around,
And the green grass grew all around.

And on that limb...there was a branch.....
And on that branch...there was a nest.....
And in that nest...there was an egg.....
And in that egg...there was a bird.....
And on that bird...there was a wing.....
And on that wing...there was a feather.....
And on that feather...there was a bug.....
And on that bug...there was a germ.......

★ WHERE IS THUMBKIN?

# April Learning Centers

## Greenhouse Center

### While playing in the Greenhouse Center children learn:

1. About growing plants through real experience.
2. To observe plants and record information about plant growth.
3. To appreciate the beauty in the world around them.
4. To develop confidence as they participate in growing plants and operating the greenhouse.

### Suggested props for the Greenhouse Center

gardening tools such as
   small shovel
   hand spade
   clippers
watering can and mister
small plastic pots and trays
potting soil
roll of clear plastic for covering the growing area
large plastic trays for catching dirt when planting or transplanting

# Curriculum Connections

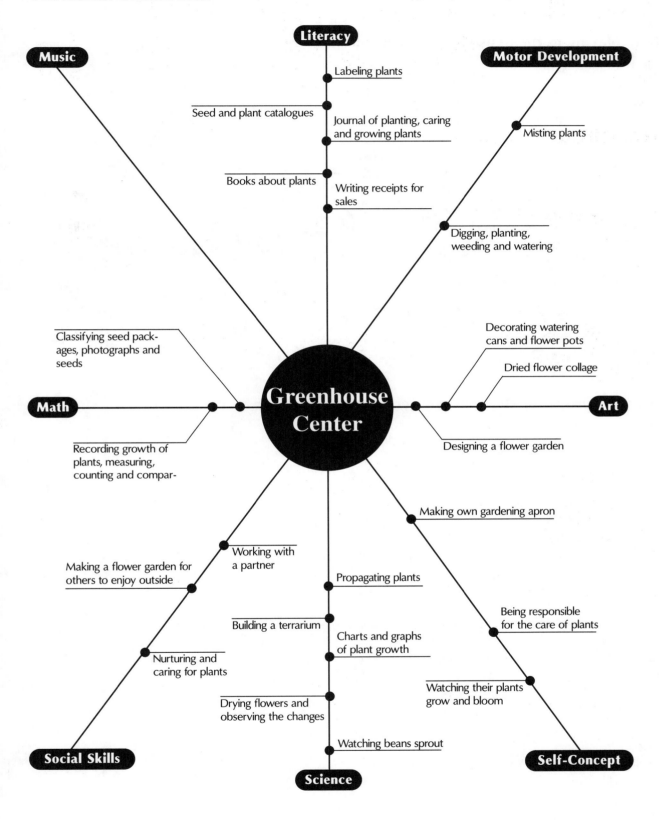

**Music**

**Literacy**
- Labeling plants
- Seed and plant catalogues
- Journal of planting, caring and growing plants
- Books about plants
- Writing receipts for sales

**Motor Development**
- Misting plants
- Digging, planting, weeding and watering

**Math**
- Classifying seed packages, photographs and seeds
- Recording growth of plants, measuring, counting and compar-

**Greenhouse Center**

**Art**
- Decorating watering cans and flower pots
- Dried flower collage
- Designing a flower garden

- Making own gardening apron
- Being responsible for the care of plants
- Watching their plants grow and bloom

**Social Skills**
- Making a flower garden for others to enjoy outside
- Working with a partner
- Nurturing and caring for plants

**Science**
- Propagating plants
- Building a terrarium
- Charts and graphs of plant growth
- Drying flowers and observing the changes
- Watching beans sprout

**Self-Concept**

★ THE COMPLETE LEARNING CENTER BOOK

# Sensory Center

## While playing in the Sensory Center children learn:

1. To understand the world in which they live.
2. To use their senses in discriminating the materials they use each day.
3. To participate in activities that will enhance their sensory abilities.
4. To use new vocabulary as they discuss the senses that they are using in the center.
5. To become more sensitive to the sights, sounds and textures of their environment.

## Suggested props for the Sensory Center

small plastic wading pool
plastic bags
materials with a variety of textures

| | |
|---|---|
| fabric | nature items |
| food items | sandpaper |
| pieces of carpet | |

items with distinctive smells, such as

| | |
|---|---|
| onion | orange |
| peppermint | soap |
| flower | perfume |
| milk | |

taste items such as dill pickle, chocolate kisses, apple pieces, pretzels, salt, sugar
visual materials

| | |
|---|---|
| paint samples | colored fabric for sorting |
| unusual pictures | sorting items in a variety of sizes |
| balls | plastic jars |
| cans | screws |
| buttons | blocks |
| books | |

ingredients for a variety of playdough recipes
cardboard boxes
trays or muffin tins for sorting
scrapbooks with magnetic pages

# Curriculum Connections

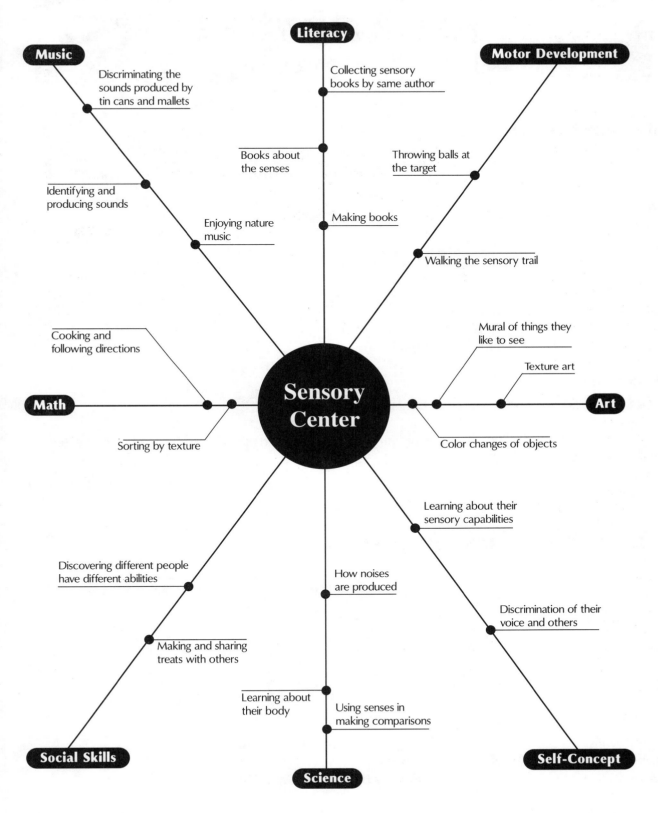

**Music**

Discriminating the sounds produced by tin cans and mallets

Identifying and producing sounds

Enjoying nature music

**Literacy**

Collecting sensory books by same author

Books about the senses

Making books

**Motor Development**

Throwing balls at the target

Walking the sensory trail

Cooking and following directions

**Math**

Sorting by texture

**Sensory Center**

Mural of things they like to see

Texture art

**Art**

Color changes of objects

Learning about their sensory capabilities

Discovering different people have different abilities

Making and sharing treats with others

**Social Skills**

How noises are produced

Learning about their body

Using senses in making comparisons

**Science**

Discrimination of their voice and others

**Self-Concept**

★ THE COMPLETE LEARNING CENTER BOOK

# Art Activities

## Walking in the Rain

**3+**

*When it's raining outside, children can create rain pictures with this activity.*

### Words to use

| | |
|---|---|
| blue | tint |
| glue | falling rain |

### Materials

| | |
|---|---|
| glue | blue food coloring |
| paper | small bowls or other containers |
| toothpicks | crayons and markers |

### What to do

1. Use blue food coloring to tint small containers of glue.
2. Ask the children to draw a picture.
3. Then suggest that they dot over the picture with toothpicks dipped into the tinted glue, creating a falling rain scene.

★ The Instant Curriculum

## Water Drop Splash Prints

**3+**

*Children learn to use an abstract shape to create an interesting print.*

### Words to use

| | |
|---|---|
| rain | sprinkel |
| splash | spot |
| drop | wet and dry |

### Materials

| | |
|---|---|
| paper towels | a variety of scraps of colored poster board |
| ball point pens | plastic bowl of water |
| scissors | *Listen to the Rain* by Bill Martin, Jr. and John Archambault |

## What to do

1. A day before the art project is to begin, put a scrap of poster board on a table and drop a few drops of water onto it. Allow the water drops to dry. They will bleach out the color in the poster board, leaving the shape of the drops of water.
2. Show the children what happened to the sheet of poster board and discuss how it happened.
3. Let them make their own Water Drop Splash Prints. Cut the poster board into strips.
4. Before letting the children make their splashes, demonstrate how to sprinkle the water without wetting the whole board.
5. Let the strips of poster board dry overnight.
6. The next day, have the children use ball point pens and draw around the water spots to emphasize their shapes.
7. Display the Water Drop Splash Prints on a bulletin board along with the book jacket from *Listen to the Rain* and a copy of the poem.

## Teaching tips

Do not be concerned if younger children lack the dexterity to draw around the shapes exactly. Let them simply make large circles around the water drop shapes. Older children may enjoy adding legs, paws, beaks or tails to create animals from the water drops.

★ MORE STORY S-T-R-E-T-C-H-E-R-S

# Rainbows                                                          3+

*Try this unique way of creating rainbows.*

## Words to use

rainbows
smear
squeegee

## Materials

small squeegee (window washer tool)
red, purple, blue, green, orange and yellow tempera paints
drawing paper

## What to do

1. The children place a small amount of each color paint on the left edge of their paper in the following order, top to bottom: purple, blue, green, yellow, orange, red.
2. The children take turns smearing paint across their paper with the squeegee to form a rainbow.

★ WHERE IS THUMBKIN?

# Designing a Flower Garden

**3+**

*When it is too early for planting outside, children can create their own indoor gardens.*

### Words to use

partner
together
label
flowers
pictures

### Materials

paper
markers and crayons
pictures of flowers (use old
    seed catalogs and seed
    packets)
ice cream sticks
box
brown paper

### What to do

1. Partners work together to select the flowers they want in their garden.
2. They glue pictures, drawings or old seed packages onto ice cream sticks.
3. Make a raised flower plot by using the top (or lid) of a box and covering it with brown paper.
4. The children stick their flower labels in this plot to create a three-dimensional flower garden plan.
5. Label these cooperatively developed flower gardens with the children's names and display in the Greenhouse Center.

★ THE COMPLETE LEARNING CENTER BOOK

# Painting Spring Flowers

**3+**

*Children learn to identify and paint a spring flower.*

### Words to use

flowers            illustrations
spring colors      identify
paint              shrubs

### Materials

*My Spring Robin* by Anne Rockwell
pink, purple, yellow tempera paints
easel
brushes
white paper

## What to do

1. Look back through *My Spring Robin* at the illustrations of spring flowers and shrubs. Help the children identify the flowers and shrubs. Also call attention to the colors.
2. Ask the children to include at least one spring flower in their paintings for today.
3. On the next day have the children include a bird in their painting. On another day, ask for paintings or drawings of spring activities the children enjoy.

## Teaching tips

Place an arrangement of spring flowers near the easel and the children will be inspired to paint with the spring colors. If you have violets, place purple, white and green paint on the easel. If you have daffodils, provide yellow and green paints.

★ More Story S-t-r-e-t-c-h-e-r-s

# Arm and Hand Tree                          3+

*Children use their arms and hands to create a tree.*

## Words to use

paint
trunk
leaves
print
branches
brown
green
bird
nest

## Materials

brown and green tempera paint
paintbrushes
sponges
paper
crayons

## What to do

1. Paint the palms of the children with brown paint. Continue painting that side of the arm up to the elbow.
2. The children press their arms and hands onto the art paper to make a print that should look like the trunk and branches of a tree. Let the prints dry.
3. Dip the sponge in the green tempera paint. "Paint" with the sponge across the branches to make leaves. The children may also want to use the sponges to make grass.
4. Older children may wish to add details like a bird's nest, bird, bug, etc. with crayons.

★ Where Is Thumbkin?

# Eggshell Mosaic

**3+**

*Children learn the value of recycling materials, even eggshells.*

## Words to use

mosaic
pattern
crush
eggshells
design
random

## Materials

dyed eggs, peeled
wax paper
rolling pin
matte board or cardboard
glue

## What to do

1. Peel dyed eggs such as those used at Easter.
2. Save the shells.
3. Place the shells on wax paper.
4. Crush the shells with a rolling pin.
5. Glue the crushed shells on matte board or cardboard.
6. Dry the project.

## Want to do more?

Color the shells of hard boiled eggs with felt pens instead of dying them. Peel these and use for the colored shells. Glue the pieces of eggshell in a definite mosaic pattern on heavy board or paper. Use tiny scraps of paper, confetti or paper punch holes in addition to the eggshell.

## Teaching tips

Young children do not always have the coordination or patience to work with picking up tiny pieces of shell. Give them a toothpick or cotton swab to dip first in glue and then touch to the shell piece. A little dot of glue on the paper will help pull the shell off the toothpick or cotton swab and onto the paper.

★ PRESCHOOL ART

# Build a Bird's Nest

*Children learn what materials one might find in a bird's nest.*

## Words to use

feathers
yarn
leaves
twigs

## Materials

empty bird's nest, if possible
green playdough
paper bags
feathers
yarn
grass
leaves
twigs
rocks
cotton

## What to do

1. If possible, show the children the real bird's nest.
2. Place the feathers, yarn, grass, leaves, twigs, rocks and cotton in different parts of the classroom.
3. Give each child a paper bag and some playdough.
4. Go on a bird nest hunt! Each child walks around the room and collects material to make a bird's nest.
5. When they are finished searching, they shape their playdough into a bird's nest.
6. Have them use the materials that they found to decorate their nest.

## Want to do more?

Talk about the homes of many kinds of animals. Talk about the types of homes that people live in. Would you like to live in a bird's nest? Why?

## Teaching tips

When each child finishes a nest, they can place bird's eggs in it. Offer a selection of colored playdough. Each child rolls small eggs from this and places the bird's eggs in their nest.

★ THE LEARNING CIRCLE

# Robin

**4+**

*Children paint, cut and glue to create a robin from a paper plate.*

## Words to use

robin
bird
tail
wing

## Materials

large paper
    plate
red paint and
    paintbrush
6" x 9" brown
    construction
    paper
markers
scissors
glue
stapler
string and dowels or sticks, optional

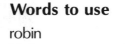

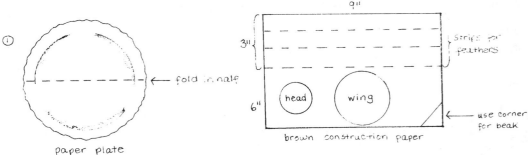

① paper plate — fold in half

9"
3"
6"
head   wing
strips for feathers
use corner for beak
brown construction paper

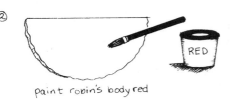

② paint robin's body red — RED

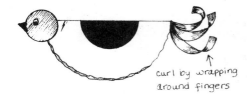

curl by wrapping around fingers

## What to do

1. Have the children fold the paper plate in half, paint it red and allow it to dry completely. This is the robin's body.
2. On brown construction paper, draw a small circle for the robin's head, a larger circle for his wings and three long strips for the tail (see illustration). Cut out each of these shapes. Allow the children to cut if they are able.
3. Glue the beak to the head. With a marker, draw an eye on each side. Glue the head to one end of the body near the top fold.
4. Fold the wing circle in half and glue it to the top center of the body fold, so you have a half circle wing on each side of the robin's body. Glue only near the fold so that the tips of the wings can be flapped up a bit.
5. Have the children curl the brown strips by wrapping them around a finger. Glue or staple them to the other end of the body near the top of the fold to finish the robin.

## Want to do more?

To make these birds fly, attach a string to the top of the bird and tie the string to the end of a stick or dowel. Take them outside and let the children fly them, but be careful of poking and running. Make a blue jay by painting the body blue and adding a blue paper crown (small fringed triangle shape) to the top of the head.

★ THE GIANT ENCYCLOPEDIA OF THEME ACTIVITIES

# Walking Puppets

*Children learn creativity and small muscle control with this exciting, fun activity.*

## Words to use

stiff
cardboard
hole
fingers
puppet
story
dramatize
tell

## Materials

child's drawing
scissors
stiff paper or cardboard
white glue

## What to do

1. Cut out a drawing and glue it to a piece of stiff paper or cardboard. (Old file folders work well.)
2. With adult help, cut two holes about one quarter inch apart at the base of the drawing. Make each hole large enough to let a finger through.
3. Put two fingers through the holes in the puppet. The fingers become the legs of the puppet.

drawing glued to file folder

cut 2 holes for fingers

## Want to do more?

Put one puppet on each hand for a show, story or play. Several artists can combine their puppets for a show with several characters.

## Teaching tips

Any size picture or any drawing can be a puppet. It is not necessary for the puppet to be an animal or a person. Even a design can be a puppet.

★ PRESCHOOL ART

APRIL

art activities

# Chalk Flowers

4+

*Chalk is fun to use on the sidewalk outside and inside with this creative activity.*

## Words to use

chalk
smudge
blend
brush
flower
shape

## Materials

soft colored chalk or pastels
colored paper and drawing paper
blossom shapes cut from old file folders
facial tissue

## What to do

1. Place a blossom shape on the colored paper.
2. Hold the shape with one hand and, with the drawing hand, trace the shape with soft colored chalk.
3. Without letting go of the shape, take a facial tissue and brush the chalk out and away from the shape.
4. When blended and brushed, remove the shape and see the flower left on the paper.
5. Continue moving and tracing with different colors. Tracings can overlap and touch or be spread out on the paper.

## Want to do more?

Simply trace and draw flower shapes instead of brushing them with the tissue. Use different shapes of flowers on one design. Color or paint the traced shapes. Where shapes overlap, make a new color such as combining red and yellow. Use shapes or stencils other than flowers. On the same sheet of paper or on a new sheet, trace around the shape with crayon, colored pencil or felt pen.

## Teaching tips

Chalk smudges and blurs are typical of this medium. Expect messy hands and elbows. One piece of facial tissue should be enough to produce several chalk flowers for each child. If desired, after the drawing is completed, an adult may spray the chalk drawings outside with hair spray or another fixative to reduce smudging. Chalkboard chalk, especially the dustless variety, does not work well for this project.

★ PRESCHOOL ART

# School Garden

**4+**

*A garden is a good metaphor for a group. Each flower is separate and beautiful yet contributes to the loveliness of the whole. Although young children are not likely to understand the connection between metaphor and reality, working together to make a common product and visibly demonstrating their togetherness makes this type of activity important.*

**APRIL**

## Words to use

group
together
individual
class
belong
unique

## Materials

a large sheet of butcher paper
several colors of construction paper
scissors
crayons
glue or paste

## What to do

1. Using different colors of construction paper, cut out a variety of stems, leaves and simple flower shapes.
2. Spread the butcher paper across the tabletop and set out the plant parts. With the children's assistance, draw the "ground" for the class garden across the length of the paper.
3. Starting at one end of the sheet, assemble the flowering plant from the cutouts by pasting them to the "ground" on the butcher paper. Write your name inside your flower. The children then take turns assembling and adding their flowers to the class garden. Each child's name should appear somewhere on his flower.
4. After all the flowers are assembled, invite the children to draw a sun, clouds, birds, bugs and butterflies in the garden.
5. Once completed, the garden can be taped to a wall or tacked to a wide bulletin board.
6. Within the next few days, conduct a circle time near the garden. Emphasize that just as each flower in a garden is special, so each child in the class is special. Point out the uniqueness of each flower.

## Want to do more?

The children can cut out the stems, leaves and flowers themselves if they are old enough to manipulate the scissors. Add decorative detail to the flowers by drawing on them with crayons.

## Home connection

Send home construction paper for parents to make "Family Gardens" with their children.

★ THE PEACEFUL CLASSROOM

# Egg Paint

**4+**

*Create bright, shiny pictures with this egg yolk paint.*

### Words to use

bright
shiny
glossy
separate
yolk
egg white
mix
paint
thick

### Materials

4 egg yolks
4 bowls
food coloring
paper
paintbrush

### What to do

1. With adult help, crack eggs and separate egg yolks from egg whites. Place one egg yolk into each bowl. Save egg whites for other art or cooking ideas.
2. Add a few drops of food coloring to each yolk and mix. Mix red, blue and yellow food coloring to make a new color in the fourth cup.
3. Paint the bright, glossy colors on the paper.

### Want to do more?

Paint on toast, hot dog buns or sugar cookies. Warm the food or bake briefly to dry the egg paint.

### Teaching tips

Use wide bowls that do not tip easily. Styrofoam grocery trays make great containers for mixing the egg yolk and food coloring. Add a few drops of water to the tray or cup if paint thickens or begins to dry before painting is complete.

★ PRESCHOOL ART

# Batik Eggs

*The process of using dye and melted wax produces beautiful (and sometimes surprising) designs.*

## Words to use

dye                    vinegar
wax                    melted
lightest              darkest

## Materials

egg carton or wrinkled aluminum foil
    for egg drying rack
hard-boiled eggs
crepe paper, several colors
scissors
bowls
hot water and tweezers
1 tablespoon white vinegar
candle, matches
paper towels
covered table

## What to do

1. Cut strips of crepe paper about one-half inch wide. Place them in a bowl. Do the same for additional colors of crepe paper.
2. An adult pours hot water on the crepe paper to release the dye. Remove the paper with tweezers or fingers. Add a tablespoon of white vinegar to set the dye. Let cool.
3. With adult help, drip candle wax onto any area of the egg. This will leave that surface the natural egg color.
4. Eggs will be decorated with several applications of wax and dye. Start by dipping the egg in the lightest color of dye first. Dry the egg with a paper towel.
5. With adult help, drip more candle wax onto the parts of the egg the artist wishes to keep a light color of dye. Dip the egg into the next darker dye and dry with a paper towel. (It may take a few minutes for the dye to become the desired color.)
6. To remove the wax, an adult places the egg on a tray covered with paper towels in a very warm oven. After the wax has melted (in about two minutes), wipe the eggs with another paper towel. Cool in an egg carton or on wrinkled aluminum foil.

## Teaching tips

This is one of those projects where the adult ends up doing most of the work so it works best as a one-on-one project; however, let the child do as much as possible. Fresh eggs can be emptied by poking a pin hole in both ends of the egg and blowing out the contents with a hefty puff of air. The contents can be used for cooking. This leaves a fragile but light, empty egg for dying. This egg will keep indefinitely.

★ PRESCHOOL ART

# Onion Skin Egg

**5+**

*Onion skins create these beautiful eggs.*

## Words to use

onion
skin
wrap
stocking
design
surprise
firmly
shine

## Materials

uncooked eggs
brown or purple onion skins
squares of old cloth or nylon
  stockings
small leaves or rice
rubber bands
pot for boiling eggs
stove
paper towels
cooking oil

① layer of onion skins
② layer of onion skins
③ layer of leaves
④ layer of onion skins
⑤ wrap cloth around the egg and skins tightly with rubber bands.

## What to do

1. Place the cloth or nylon stocking square on the table. Put about six layers of onion skin on the cloth. Place leaves or bits of rice on top of the onion skins.
2. Place the egg on top of the skins, leaves and rice. Place more onion skins on top of this.
3. Wrap the cloth or nylon stocking around the egg and skins firmly. Wrap several rubber bands around the cloth to keep it in place and to press the onion skins firmly against the egg's surface.
4. With adult help, lower the wrapped egg into a pot of boiling water for about 30 minutes. Remove the egg from the pot and cool. Remove the cloth and materials from the egg.
5. Rub the egg with a little cooking oil to give it a shine.

## Teaching tips

Young children usually need help wrapping the egg firmly in the nylon stocking.

★ PRESCHOOL ART

# Marbling

**5+**

*Children love to create their own marbled paper.*

## Words to use

marbling
ink
swirl
pattern
float

## Materials

waterproof inks, variety of colors
large Styrofoam grocery trays
plastic spoons
light color blotting paper
apron
newspaper covered drying area

## What to do

1. Fill the grocery trays halfway with water.
2. Gently drop a small amount of water-proof ink onto the surface of the water. Add drops of additional colors.
3. Stir the ink over the water with a plastic spoon slowly and carefully. (The ink will swirl and float forming beautiful patterns.)
4. With adult help, place the blotting paper on top of the floating colors for about thirty seconds.
5. With adult help, quickly lift the paper, turn it over and hold it flat to stop the colors from running.
6. Dry the colored paper on a flat, covered surface. This project can take several days to dry.

## Want to do more?

This project is very pretty to watch using a clear glass bowl with a piece of plain white paper beneath the bowl. Skip the paper printing step and just enjoy watching the colors swirl and mix in the bowl.

## Teaching tips

Using small squares of paper makes this project easier to control. Adult supervision is necessary when working with waterproof ink, both using it and cleaning it up.

★ PRESCHOOL ART

# Circle Time and Group Activities

## It Rained a Mist

**3+**

*This activity develops coordination.*

### Words to use

mist
rain
grow
bloom
act out

### Materials

### What to do

This poem is an American folk song which is wonderful to act out.

> *It rained a mist, it rained a mist,*
> *It rained all over the town, town, town.*
> *It rained all over the town. (children wiggle their fingers like falling rain)*
>
> *The sun came out, the sun came out,*
> *It shone all over the town, town, town.*
> *It shone all over the town. (children put their arms over their heads for the sun)*
>
> *And then the grass began to grow,*
> *It grew all over the town, town, town.*
> *It grew all over the town. (children crouch down and pretend to grow)*
>
> *And then the flowers began to bloom,*
> *They bloomed all over the town, town, town.*
> *They bloomed all over the town. (children pretend to bloom like flowers)*

★ 500 FIVE MINUTE GAMES

# A Little Sun

*This fingerplay, which develops small muscle control and coordination, is an enjoyable addition to circle time.*

## Words to use

| | |
|---|---|
| flowers | soil |
| water | sunlight |
| roots | stem |
| leaves | blossoms |

## Materials

## What to do

1. During circle time talk about what flowers need to grow—soil, water and sunlight. Talk about the parts of a flower—roots, stem, leaves, blossom petals.
2. Do the following fingerplay with the children.

> *"A Little Sun"*
>
> *A little sun, (hold arms above head)*
> *A little rain, (wiggle fingers in the air in a downward motion)*
> *Now pull up all the weeds. (pretend to pull weeds)*
> *Our flowers grow, all in a row (hold up all ten fingers lined up like flowers)*
> *From tiny little seeds. (hold thumb and finger to show size of seeds)*

3. Encourage the children to do the motions of the fingerplay with you.
4. Repeat frequently so the children can practice the fingerplay.

## Want to do more?

**Dramatic play**: Set up a flower shop in the dramatic play area. Provide flower catalogs; silk, plastic and real flowers; orange juice cans (to hold flowers); telephone; pads of paper and pencils; aprons; cash register and play money.

**Field trips**: Visit a flower shop in the area. Take a walk in the neighborhood and look for different kinds of flowers.

**Math**: Make a memory game using two identical nursery catalogs. Cut out identical pictures and glue the pictures on index cards.

## Books to read

*My Garden Grows* by Aldren Watson
*The Reason for a Flower* by Ruth Heller
*What Is a Flower* by Jennifer W. Day

★ THE GIANT ENCYCLOPEDIA OF CIRCLE TIME AND GROUP ACTIVITIES

# Seeds

**3+**

*Teaches children about plant growth.*

## Words to use

garden
seeds
row
water
roots
buttercup

## Materials

## What to do

Try acting out this poem to reinforce a discussion about planting.

> *I work in my garden,*
> *I plant seeds in a row.*
> *The rain and the sunshine*
> *Will help my seeds grow.*
> *Sometimes the weather*
> *Is dry and hot,*
> *So I sprinkle the earth*
> *With my watering pot.*
> *The roots push downward,*
> *The stems push up,*
> *Soon I will see a buttercup.*

★ 500 FIVE MINUTE GAMES

# Sing a Song of Spring

**3+**

*This activity helps children learn about the first signs of Spring.*

## Words to use

sign
grass
flowers
tree buds
birds
nest

## Materials

grass
flowers
tree buds
bird's nest (use only an abandoned nest, if available)

## What to do

1. At circle time talk about and show the children the signs of spring including grass, flowers, tree buds and an abandoned bird's nest, if available.
2. Sing the following song with the children to the tune of "London Bridge."

> *All the grass is turning green, turning green, turning green,*
> *All the grass is turning green; it is springtime.*

Other verses:

> *See the birdies build their nest....*
> *All the flowers are blooming....*
> *Trees are budding everywhere....*

★ THE GIANT ENCYCLOPEDIA OF CIRCLE TIME AND GROUP ACTIVITIES

# Growing Flowers                                3+

*Understanding the needs of living things is a prerequisite for caretaking. Gentleness is based on respect and appreciation. A simple activity involving the care of a plant is a good way to begin.*

## Words to use

life
growing up
care
gentle
respect
appreciation

## Materials

flowering potted plant

## What to do

1. Show the plant to children. Talk about what the plant needs to grow. Emphasize the importance of being gentle when touching the flower. What would happen if someone grabbed or slapped it? Invite the children to touch and smell the flower gently, one at a time.
2. Talk to the children about how a flower grows from a tiny seed. Begin with the planting of the seed, then describe watering, sprouting and stem and leaf growth.

3. Act out the following fingerplay with the children:

> *Tiny seed planted just right,*
> *Not a breath of air, nor a ray of light. (cover right fist with left hand)*
> *Rain falls slowly to and fro,*
> *And now the seed begins to grow. (remove left hand and slowly uncurl*
>    *right fist)*
> *Slowly reaching for the light*
> *With all its energy, all its might. (right hand makes creeping motion upward with*
>    *fingers together)*
> *The little seed's work is almost done,*
> *To grow up tall and face the sun. (stretch out fingers of right hand)*

## Want to do more?

With older children, pass the plant around the circle. Emphasize being gentle. Ask the children to bring a potted plant from home to show the group. Compare two plants with different needs for sun and water, for example, a cactus and a philodendron.

## Home connection

Encourage parents to give their children the responsibility of caring for a potted plant at home. They should make sure their children understand what to do to care properly for the plant.

★ THE PEACEFUL CLASSROOM

# Plant a Little Seed                3+

*This poem teaches about growth.*

## Words to use

poem
act out

## Materials

## What to do

Act out the following poem.

> *Dig a little hole.*
> *Plant a little seed.*
> *Pour on a little water.*
> *Pull a little weed.*

*Give a little sunshine,*
*And before you know,*
*Your little seed will be a plant,*
*And grow, grow, grow.*

*Flowers, flowers, flowers,*
*Hurry up, hurry up.*
*Flowers, flowers, flowers,*
*Grow, grow, grow.*

★ 500 FIVE MINUTE GAMES

# Plant Brainstorms                                3+

*This activity encourages thinking skills.*

## Words to use

questions
answers
where
how
what

## Materials

white poster board
felt pens, crayons
two large plastic eyes
glue

## What to do

1. Draw a large plant on the poster board and color it. Glue two plastic eyes on the plant. Display it at the Learning Circle. Learn the Plant Brainstorm questions.
2. To help the children learn about plants and gain an appreciation for them, invite a brainstorm with the following questions. If necessary, help the children to think of possible answers.
✔ Where do plants grow? (oceans, lakes, deserts, mountains, gardens, on rocks, on wood and in snow!)
✔ How can we tell that plants are alive? (We can watch them grow! Vines twist and turn their stems. They grow towards the sun. Buds open into flowers. They fight for ground space! Weeds can overtake a garden.)
✔ What kind of food do plants make? (potatoes, carrots, beets, cucumbers, watermelons, strawberries)
✔ What happens to a plant when you pull it from the ground? (It will die unless you put in into a pot with soil and water.)
✔ How can we keep a plant healthy? (Give the plant the right amount of water, sunshine and food. Be gentle when touching a plant. Spray the plant with bug spray if insects are harming it.)

★ THE LEARNING CIRCLE

# What a Storm!

**4+**

*In this activity children create their own "thunderstorm."*

### Words to use

thunder
storm
lightening
loud
soft
dark
clouds

### Materials

*Thunderstorm* by Mary Szilagyi
drum

### What to do

1. At circle time read *Thunderstorm* and talk about the story.
2. Review how the storm began, developed and ended.
3. Introduce the idea of making a storm in the classroom by beginning to rub your hands together making a soft sound. Tell the class to imagine that it is beginning to rain softly. Continue the development of the storm by snapping fingers. Follow this by patting your legs. Reverse the actions to have the storm subside.
4. Ask the children to follow your actions in making a storm. Begin, develop and end the storm. Add thunder by asking a child to beat the drum at a given signal. Drum beats should be soft at the beginning of the storm, louder as it develops and soft again as it subsides.

### Want to do more?

**Language:** Record parts of a real thunderstorm and ask the children to listen to the tape. Encourage the children to describe the storm using descriptive words.

**Music:** Use rhythm instruments to develop and end the storm. Sand blocks may be used to begin, then rhythm sticks followed by tone blocks to develop the storm. As the storm subsides, reverse the sequence.

### Books to read

*Rain, Drop, Splash* by Alvin Tresselt
*Thunder Cake* by Patricia Polacco

★ THE GIANT ENCYCLOPEDIA OF CIRCLE TIME AND GROUP ACTIVITIES

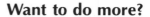
circle time activities

# I'm Listening to the Rain

**4+**

*This activity encourages children to develop good listening skills.*

## Words to use

recording
rain
pretend
hear
listen

## Materials

recording of rain

## What to do

1. At circle time talk about rain and explain to the children that you have a recording of the sound of rain that you would like them to listen to.
2. Ask the children to close their eyes and listen to the recording of the rain.
3. After listening to the recording, talk about the sound of rain. Tell the children to pretend that they are outside walking in the rain. What do they hear (thunder, wind)? Do cars sound different in the rain (windshield wipers, tires on wet roads)? Can they hear the splashing when they walk in puddles? Can they hear birds chirping in the rain? Ask the children to tell about an experience they had in the rain.

## Books to read

*Rain* by Peter Spiers
*Rain Talk* by Mary Serfozo

★ THE GIANT ENCYCLOPEDIA OF CIRCLE TIME AND GROUP ACTIVITIES

# Seed to Flower Rhyme Play

**4+**

*Children learn about how seeds grow while they act out this poem.*

## Words to use

seeds
ground
rain
sun
shoot
bud
flower

## Materials

## What to do

The children change from seeds to flowers as they say the following poem.

> In spring there was a little seed, sleeping in the ground,
>    (children pretend to be asleep)
> In the sky there were gray clouds and rain was coming down.
>    (tap floor for raindrop sound)
> Water made the seed wake up, before it could get dry,
>    (children pretend to wake up)
> Pushing up to see the sun, so big up in the sky.
>    (turn head upward while standing up)
> First a little shoot popped out, (jump up)
> Then one by one leaves grew. (lift one arm, then the other, as leaves)
> And last, a bud became a flower,
>    (move hands with fingers fanned out to frame face)
> And Nature smiles at me and you. (children "draw" a smile on their faces, point
>    to themselves and then to others)

★ THE GIANT ENCYCLOPEDIA OF CIRCLE TIME AND GROUP ACTIVITIES

# Class Garden                                              4+

*The Class Garden should be a shared, group effort. Instead of one child digging, planting, watering and weeding one plant, each child should have some responsibility for a large area if not the entire garden.*

## Words to use

cooperate
teamwork
seeds
growth
nurture
caretaker
environment
responsibilities

## Materials

seeds
garden tools
small green trees cut from green construction paper, one for each child
poster board
marker

## What to do

1. Just before planting time arrives, have a circle time near the spot where your garden will be. Talk about seeds and growth. How does the earth nurture a seed so it grows? What do plants need to survive when they appear? Talk about what it means to be a caretaker or steward of the environment.
2. Discuss garden plans with the group. Where will the garden be? What kinds of plants will it contain? Use plants that mature early in the growing season. Show them the pictures on the seed packets. Make a list of all the tasks required on a poster board. This will become the assignment board.
3. Go to the art area and help the children decorate and write their names on the small green tree shapes.
4. Ask the children to bring their trees back to circle time. Set up the poster board. Go over the responsibilities involved in beginning the garden. Engage the children in deciding what they will do. Tape each child's tree next to her assignment on the board.
5. Change responsibilities and make adjustments on the assignment board as your garden progresses.

## Want to do more?

When the garden begins to mature, take Polaroid pictures to give the children.

## Home connection

Encourage parents to start a small family garden or indoor potted plant arrangement. Family members can share responsibilities for the plants.

★ THE PEACEFUL CLASSROOM

circle time activities

# Dramatic Play Activities

## Yellow Rain Slickers and Other Rain Wear          3+

*Children learn to dress themselves in rain wear and to improvise "walking in the rain" play episodes.*

### Words to use

| | |
|---|---|
| raincoat | slickers |
| rain hats | boots |
| umbrellas | play |
| dramatize | imagine |
| pretend | book |
| story | characters |

### Materials

*A Walk in the Rain* by Ursel Scheffler
four or five sets of rain wear, such as slickers, raincoats,
  rain hats, boots, umbrellas

### What to do

1. Ask parents to send in umbrellas, boots, extra rain-coats and slickers that older children have outgrown, including some in adult sizes that can be cut off.
2. Place the rain gear in the housekeeping and dress-up corner. Remind children of how to play safely with umbrellas.
3. Read *A Walk in the Rain*. Begin the play session by pretending to be Josh's grandmother who loves to walk in the rain.
4. After a brief time, leave the children to play on their own.

### Teaching tips

The props, such as the rain slickers, serve as a stimulus for the children to role play activities associated with them and with the book. You only need four or five sets of rainwear, not enough for each child in the class because only four or five children are in the dramatic play center at one time.

★ MORE STORY S-T-R-E-T-C-H-E-R-S

# Gardening Apron

*This useful apron can be easily made by the children.*

## Words to use

waterproof
apron
protect
keep clean

## Materials

large green bags
scissors
string or yarn

## What to do

1. Transform large green garbage bags into waterproof gardening aprons.
2. Cut a hole in the bottom of the garbage bags for the child's head and slits in the sides for arm holes.
3. Cut an additional slit from the center of the opening for the head, down to the open end of the back of the bag so the child can slip the gardening apron on without having to pull the plastic bag over the head.
4. The children wear these when planting and watering.
5. If necessary, secure the apron with string or yarn tied around the bag, at the waist.

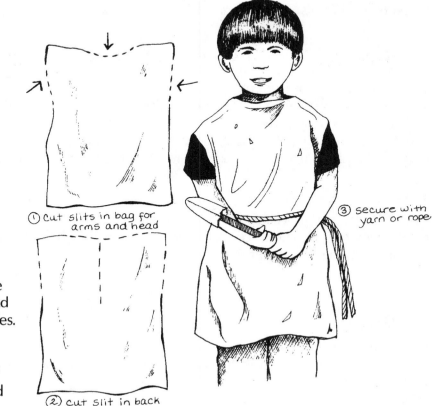

① Cut slits in bag for arms and head

② Cut slit in back

③ secure with yarn or rope

★ THE COMPLETE LEARNING CENTER BOOK

# Gardening Clothes

*Children learn to dress in clothing that they are not used to wearing.*

## Words to use

canning
hoeing
gardening
planting

raking
catalogs
growing

## Materials

| | |
|---|---|
| jeans | *This Year's Garden* by Cynthia Rylant |
| shirts | straw hats |
| caps | gloves |
| seed catalogs | seed packages |
| home canned foods | watering can |

## What to do

1. Collect the clothing, catalogs and home canned foods from supplies in the classroom, your household and donations from parents.
2. Help the children begin to sort and arrange their farm house to get ready for the gardening season.
3. Read the book. Start the play by pretending to be Granny who is looking at the seed catalog and says she doesn't want to plant so many beans this year because she is tired of canning.
4. After the play is underway, quietly leave the group to their own play themes.

## Teaching tips

Dramatic play is a marvelous time for children to try on new roles, and with each new role comes an opportunity to try on new vocabulary, to say words they have never said before, such as "canning," "raking," "hoeing," "catalogs."

★ More Story S-t-r-e-t-c-h-e-r-s

# I Found It                                   3+

*This activity encourages children to develop observation skills and early reading skills.*

## Words to use

| | |
|---|---|
| rebus | picture |
| find | look |

## Materials

butcher paper or any long piece of paper
catalogs or magazines
scissors
glue
paper and marker

## What to do

1. The children create a large mural to cover one of the Sensory Center walls. They cut pictures out of catalogs or magazines that show items that they like to see. Let the children glue pictures to the mural for several days or until the mural is full.
2. The teacher places a sign by the mural that says, for example, "Do you see 👁 👁 a tree 🌲 ?"
3. The children try to find a tree on the mural.
4. After a few days, put a new sign up asking the children to look for a different item, or ask a child to look for a specific picture. These searches can become more difficult over time.

★ The Complete Learning Center Book

APRIL

dramatic play activities

# Language Activities

## Pen Pals

**3+**

*This activity helps children recognize that words are written speech.*

### Words to use

letter
message
write
send
deliver
read

### Materials

envelopes
paper
crayons, markers

### What to do

1. Keep a supply of envelopes readily available for children.
2. Encourage children to draw pictures that tell their friend something or to use inventive spelling to convey a message. Children can also use the teacher as a scribe.
3. When letters are complete, have children put them in envelopes and deliver them to their friends' cubby holes.

★ THE INSTANT CURRICULUM

## Rain Sayings

**3+**

*Builds children's weather vocabulary.*

### Words to use

| | |
|---|---|
| pitter | rain |
| patter | fall |
| window | wet |

**Materials**

**What to do**

Poems are a wonderful way to increase children's vocabulary.

> *Pitter, patter, pitter, patter,*
> *Listen to the rain.*
> *Pitter, patter, pitter, patter,*
> *On my windowpane.*
>
> *Evening red and morning gray*
> *Are the signs of a bonny day.*
> *Evening gray and morning red*
> *Bring down rain on the farmer's head.*

★ 500 Five Minute Games

# Rain Poem

**3+**

*This activity practices memory skills.*

**Words to use**

| | |
|---|---|
| rain | trees |
| rooftop | me |

**Materials**

**What to do**

1. This popular poem lends itself to practicing memory skills and experiencing language.

> *Rain on the green grass,*
> *Rain on the trees,*
> *Rain on the rooftops,*
> *But not on me.*

2. Let the children name three things on which it rains, for example, sidewalk, kitten and window.
3. Repeat the poem, inserting these three things.

> *Rain on the sidewalk,*
> *Rain on the kitten,*
> *Rain on the windows,*
> *But not on me.*

4. Always end with "But not on me." This can get pretty silly!

★ 500 Five Minute Games

# The Parts of a Tree                                      3+

*Children learn to listen for the cues for when to add the flannel board pieces of the tree.*

## Words to use

green
grass
hole
ground
tree
roots
limb
branch
twig
nest
egg
bird
feather
story
flannel board
sing
retell

## Materials

*The Green Grass Grows All Around,* A Traditional
  Folk Song illustrated by Hilde Hoffman
flannel board pieces to represent a patch of green
  grass, a hole in the ground, tree roots, limb,
  branch, twig, nest, egg, bird, feather

## What to do

1. Demonstrate *The Green Grass Grows All Around* by reading the folk song or singing it while putting up the parts of the tree at the appropriate cue.
2. Read or sing again and have a child place the flannel board pieces on.
3. Leave the flannel board pieces and the book on display in the library corner as a part of your spring emphasis.

## Teaching tips

For variety, try a backwards version of the song, "There was a feather, the prettiest little feather you ever did see, and with this feather, there was a bird," etc.

★ Story S-t-r-e-t-c-h-e-r-s

# Book of Our Favorite Spring Flowers and Birds    3+

*Children learn to describe, draw and write about their favorite spring flowers and birds.*

### Words to use

| | |
|---|---|
| spring | flowers |
| colors | bind |
| book | draw |

### Materials

*My Spring Robin* by Anne Rockwell
heavy white typing paper or construction paper
colored pencils or markers
ruler
pencils

### What to do

1. With the small group who choose the library center, begin discussing their favorite spring flowers and birds. Encourage them to use specific colors, as rosy stripes on a white flower.
2. Make a one-inch margin along the left hand side of the paper by drawing a line from the top of the page to the bottom. Ask the children not to draw in the margin because it will be covered when the book is bound.
3. Let the children draw and write about their favorite spring flowers and birds.
4. Bind the children's illustrations and writings into a class book to place in the library corner. (See page 258 for binding instruction.)

### Teaching tips

Share the children's books at group time and compare the children's favorite flowers and birds with those found in *My Spring Robin*.

★ MORE STORY S-T-R-E-T-C-H-E-R-S

# Seed and Gardening Catalogs    3+

*Children learn to select favorite pictures of fruits, vegetables, flowers, trees and shrubs, and to use descriptive words.*

### Words to use

| | |
|---|---|
| catalog | fruits |
| vegetables | flowers |
| shrubs | trees |

## Materials

variety of seed and plant catalogs

## What to do

1. Place the catalogs on the library shelves alongside the books on plants and gardening which you have selected for this unit.
2. Interact with the children, telling them some of your favorite fruits, such as "granny apples," "big boy tomatoes," "purple dwarf iris," "camellia shrubs" and "silver maple trees."
3. Encourage the children to select fruits, vegetables, flowers, shrubs and trees they like. As they read and look at the pictures, take time to read aloud some of the descriptions.
4. After a few days of the children looking at and reading the catalogs, let them begin to predict what the text might say to describe the plant. They can think of descriptive words by looking at the pictures.

## Teaching tips

Make the covers of the catalogs more durable by covering them with clear contact paper and taping over the places where the staples hold the pages together. For younger children, roll a strip of clear tape along the edge of each page so they can grasp this edge to turn the pages more easily.

★ MORE STORY S-T-R-E-T-C-H-E-R-S

# Flower Colors Match Up                                  3+

*Children develop their cognitive color skills by using these picture cards.*

## Words to use

color words
flowers
match

## Materials

nursery catalogs
poster board
scissors
markers
ruler
clear contact paper
white glue
reclosable bag

## What to do

1. Cut out 3" squares of different pictures of flowers.
2. Cut poster board into 3" squares.
3. Glue flower pictures to poster board squares and let dry.

4. Cut more poster board into 2-1/2" x 5" pieces.
5. Print "RED" with a red marker on one card, "BLUE" with a blue on a second, "YELLOW" in dark yellow on a third, and so on.
6. Cover front and back of all pieces with clear contact paper. Use a reclosable bag to store the game.
7. Invite the children to compare the different colored flower cards to one another.
8. Encourage them to match all the blue flower cards to the "BLUE" card, yellow flower cards to the "YELLOW" card, etc.

## Want to do more?

This is a good manipulative table top game to set out during a week on spring, gardens or flowers. Encourage children to draw or paint a picture of what their garden might look like.

## Book to read

*Little Blue and Little Yellow* by Leo Lionni

★ THE GIANT ENCYCLOPEDIA OF THEME ACTIVITIES

# Puppet Party

# 3+

*Encourages children's creativity and language skills.*

## Words to use

| | |
|---|---|
| puppet | puppet show |
| story | faces |
| talk | dialogue |
| characters | beginning |
| middle | end |
| plot | |

## Materials

paper plates
paper
crayons
glue
tongue depressors

## What to do

1. The children draw faces on the plates and decorate the faces to create a puppet face. Glue tongue depressors on the plates for handles.
2. The children, in pairs, present puppet shows for the group.
3. Be aware that young children may not be capable of creating a plot, so any dialogue created is acceptable.

★ THE INSTANT CURRICULUM

# Spider Puppets

**4+**

*Use these spiders to act out "The Eensy Weensy Spider."*

### Words to use

spider          legs
eight           move
act out

### Materials

pipe cleaners
elastic string

### What to do

1. The children create spider puppets from pipe cleaners by twisting four pipe cleaners together in the middle and spreading the eight resulting legs. Attach a piece of elastic string for a great effect.
2. Let the children create their own versions of movements for the "Eensy Weensy Spider" song, or let them create their own story.

★ Where Is Thumbkin?

# Pick a Pair

**4+**

*This activity can be challenging for some children, but it will encourage all children to use their listening skills.*

### Words to use

sounds
pictures
match
order
familiar
know
listen
hear

### Materials

tape recorder and empty tape
magazines
scissors
paper
glue

## What to do

1. Make a tape of several sounds—some difficult and some less difficult. Example: door bell, telephone ring, fire engine, dog barking, baby crying, laughter, etc.
2. Cut pictures from magazines to represent each sound.
3. Glue each picture on construction paper.
4. The children listen to the tape and arrange the pictures in the same order as the sounds were heard on the tape.

★ THE INSTANT CURRICULUM

# What's in a Bird's Nest?                    4+

*This reading readiness activity allows children to discover the materials used in a bird's nest.*

## Words to use

| | |
|---|---|
| nest | build |
| natural materials | mud |
| sticks | string |

## Materials

| | |
|---|---|
| bird's nest(s) | poster board |
| glue or tape | marker |
| newspaper | |

## What to do

1. When trees are bare, bird nests are easy to find. Ask parents to become "nature detectives" in the hunt for abandoned nests. Keep the nest for this activity.
2. Prepare a table or the floor by covering the area with newspaper.
3. Allow a group of children to disassemble the bird nest. After each discovery of the material used, glue or tape the item on the poster board. The teacher can label each find.
4. The poster can then be displayed on the science table with any leftover portions of the nest.
5. Make sure everyone washes hands thoroughly!

## Want to do more?

Make bird feeders. String cereal on yarn, tie the ends together and hang for the birds to enjoy! Give each child two ribbons of crepe paper for wings. Play a recording of "Feed the Birds" from "Mary Poppins." Direct the children to move their wings to the music. Give positional directions: above your head, behind your tail, etc.

## Books to read

*Are You My Mother?* by P.D. Eastman
*Dead Bird* by Margaret Wise Brown
*Fly Away Home* by Eve Bunting
*The Best Nest* by P.D. Eastman

★ THE GIANT ENCYCLOPEDIA OF THEME ACTIVITIES

# Math Activities

## Heavy/Light

**3+**

*Children learn measurement concepts.*

### Words to use

heavy   scale
light    pounds
sort     compare
weigh

### Materials

heavy and light classroom items
classroom scale

### What to do

1. The children hold the items and sort them into heavy and light categories.
2. Bring out the scale and let the children weigh the items.
3. Ask the children if elephants are heavy or light.

★ WHERE IS THUMBKIN?

## Those That Are Alike

**3+**

*Children learn to group and sort, classification skills.*

### Words to use

sort
match
color
same
different

### Materials

old seed packages
pictures of plants from plant catalogs and magazines
basket

## What to do

1. Cut out pictures of plants from old seed packages, plant catalogs and magazines.
2. Place this collection in a gardening basket in the Greenhouse Center.
3. The children group the pictures of flowers by color or another characteristic they identify for classification.

★ The Complete Learning Center Book

# Spring Flower Puzzles                                       3+

*Children learn to use fine motor coordination to reassemble photos of flowers.*

## Words to use

puzzle
shapes
fit together
pieces
cut out
assemble

## Materials

magazine, calendar or seed catalog pictures of flowering trees, shrubs and flowers
thin cardboard or poster board
glue or rubber cement
scissors
masking tape
plastic bags

## What to do

1. Let the children at the mathematics and manipulatives center select and cut out pictures of favorite spring plants.
2. Cut pieces of thin cardboard the sizes of the pictures.
3. Use rubber cement or glue to attach pictures onto the cardboard. Let dry for a few hours.
4. Draw random puzzle shapes onto the backs of the cardboard.
5. Cut puzzle pieces.
6. Store in large plastic bags. Make a label from masking tape and print the name of the flower or plant on the label.

## Teaching tips

Ask parents to save cardboard backs from tablets and legal pads. Poster board and cardboard from gift boxes can also be used.

★ More Story S-t-r-e-t-c-h-e-r-s

# Elephant Patterns

*In this activity, children learn patterning skills.*

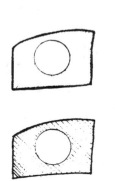

cut several of each color red, yellow and green.

APRIL

## Words to use

patterns
order
same
copy

## Materials

elephants cut from gray felt
several felt saddles in red, blue, yellow and green
flannel board

## What to do

1. The children place the animals on the flannel board and then create patterns by placing the saddles on elephants' backs.
2. Create patterns that the children can copy or continue.

★ WHERE IS THUMBKIN?

math activities

# Match Makers

**3+**

*Encourages children to develop good listening skills and the skill of ordering.*

## Words to use

cans        put inside
shake       loudest
softest

## Materials

3-4 cans with lids
assorted objects that fit into the cans

## What to do

1. Provide the children with three or four cans with lids, for example, potato chip cans or coffee cans, and a box of objects that can fit into the cans.
2. The children put objects in the cans.
3. Then they shake the cans to determine which cans make the loudest sound, which cans make the softest sound.
4. Encourage the children to order the cans from softest to loudest sound.

★ THE INSTANT CURRICULUM

# Feeding the Elephant

**4+**

*Children learn one-to-one correspondence, numeral recognition and counting.*

## Words to use

numeral
count
peanut
elephant
sequence

## Materials

peanuts
cut-out elephants

## What to do

1. Put numerals 1-10 on the elephants.
2. Encourage the children to count the appropriate number of peanuts for each elephant, 1 to 10.
3. Younger children can match one elephant to one peanut.
4. Older children can sequence the elephants numerically.

★ WHERE IS THUMBKIN?

# Seed Wheel

*Children practice their observation skills by matching real seeds. This is an excellent activity to complement a gardening unit in the spring.*

## Words to use

seed
wheel
match

## Materials

12" cardboard circle (can be obtained at pizza shop) divided into 12 equal pie-shaped wedges using a black felt marker
12 different kinds of seeds, flower or vegetable
12 wooden spring clothespins
tacky glue

attach seeds to bottom of clothespins and match the seeds to like seeds on the wheel.

*(Seed wheel labeled: Morning Glory, Apple, Marigold, Squash, Dandelion, Watermelon, Corn, Cherry, Bean, Daisy, Sunflower, Pumpkin)*

## What to do

1. Glue one seed in the middle of each section of the cardboard and label that section with the name of the seed.
2. Glue an identical seed to the top of the snapping end of one clothespin.
3. Continue Steps 1 and 2 until you have 12 different seeds on the circle and 12 matching seeds on the clothespins.
4. Read the children a story about seeds (see suggested books below).
5. Let the children look at seeds and seed packets.
6. Show the children the seed wheel and clothespins. Tell the children that they are to match two seeds that are the same by clipping a clothespin onto the section of the seed wheel that matches.

## Want to do more?

Put out a bowl of mixed seeds (don't use very tiny ones) and let the children sort them. Make several seed wheels using different kinds of seeds. Store each wheel with its own clothespins, and allow the children to use them independently.

## Books to read

*How a Seed Grows* by Helene Jordan
*How Does My Garden Grow?* by William and Elizabeth Benton
*The Riddle of Seeds* by W. Hammond (Teachers' Information Book)
*What Shall I Put in the Hole That I Dig?* by Eleanor Thompson
*Where Does Your Garden Grow?* by Augusta Goldin

★ THE GIANT ENCYCLOPEDIA OF THEME ACTIVITIES

# Crunchy Sets 4+

*A tasty way to learn about sets and practice sorting and counting skills.*

## Words to use

crackers
alike
different
count
sort

## Materials

assorted crackers

## What to do

1. At snack time give children a handful of different shaped crackers; ask them to separate the crackers into sets by shape.
2. Ask children to count the number of crackers in each set.
3. Each child eats her own crackers for snack.

★ THE INSTANT CURRICULUM

# Two Feet Long 4+

*Children learn measuring skills.*

## Words to use

trace          foot
measure        cut out
cardboard      stiff
as long as

## Materials

cardboard
marker
scissors

## What to do

1. Each child traces around her foot on a piece of cardboard or tag board.
2. Cut out the foot shape. (Adult help may be needed.)
3. Show the children how to use their own foot to measure the length of the room, the art table, etc.

★ THE INSTANT CURRICULUM

# What Color Is Spring?

*Spring is a wonderful annual event. It is a time of new life, growth, sweet smells, warmth and love. There are many new colors that suddenly appear following the bitter cold and dreariness of a long winter. These are the colors of spring. This activity helps the children develop an awareness of the sights and colors of spring and lets them use their observing and recording skills.*

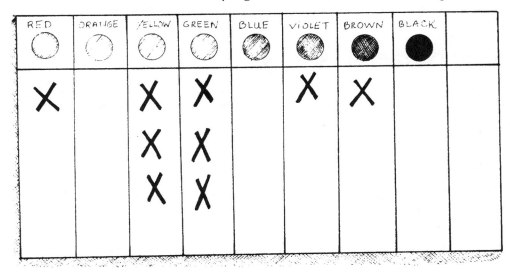

## Words to use

names of colors
collect
mark
seasons

## Materials

box of crayons
tagboard divided into columns with one each of the following colors at the top of each column: red, orange, yellow, green, blue, violet, brown and black—keep one column open for colors that do not match those presented

## What to do

1. Make a color tally card for each child. Tagboard should be divided into eight columns (see illustration). Each column is for recording one color. Children can help make the tally cards by coloring the top of each column with a different color.
2. Discuss spring. When does it come? What changes take place? What new sounds do we hear? What new colors do we see? Photographs, as well as real objects such as grass or a daffodil may be helpful.
3. Take a walk in the spring. Let each child take a color tally card. Each time the child sees a specific color he or she makes a mark in the column under that color.
4. Upon return to the home or classroom, the children will have a record of the colors of spring that they have observed.
5. Discuss the colors. Compare the tally cards; did everyone find the same colors?

### Want to do more?

Take a color walk during each of the seasons. Check the colors of the seasons against each other. What color differences do you notice? Why do colors change from season to season? Which season has the most colors? Which season has the least colors? Which season has the most yellow, the most blue, etc.? Using pictures from magazines or collections of sticks, grass, leaves, buds, etc., make a collage for each season. Keep and compare.

★ Hug a Tree

# Magnetic Numerals with Rhymes                                4+

*Through this activity, children practice counting, recognizing numerals, associating number names, matching sets and, in addition, they practice their listening skills.*

## Words to use

match                    mother
babies                   numerals

## Materials

magnetic board           *Over in the Meadow* by Olive A. Wadsworth
magnetic numerals        pictures of the mother animals and insects
magnetic strips          pictures of the sets of baby animals and insects from *Over in the Meadow*

## What to do

1. Working with small groups of children at a time, have them match the pictures of mother animals or insects and their babies.
2. Ask a child who can count from one to five to arrange the numerals in order on the magnetic board.
3. Have another child arrange the numerals from six to ten.
4. Remove the numerals and put them back up one at a time as you read the book.
5. Mix up the pictures of the mothers and the babies and give each child several.
6. Read *Over in the Meadow*. When you say the name and number of an animal or insect, the child with the picture of the mother attaches it to the magnetic board, and the child with the picture of the set of baby animals attaches it alongside.

★ Story S-t-r-e-t-c-h-e-r-s

# Target Practice                                              5+

*What a fun way to learn about numbers!*

## Words to use

target
toss
bounce

## Materials

milk cartons
scissors
stapler
markers
yarn balls or tennis balls

## What to do

1. Cut the top off milk cartons on an angle at different heights, then staple the sides together to form a target with three or four sections. Numbers can be printed on the sections.
2. Have children toss a yarn ball or bounce tennis balls into the target sections and add up the points.

★ THE INSTANT CURRICULUM

# Egg Carton Shake

**5+**

*Shake your way to math skills!*

## Words to use

dots
all together
shake
carton

count
add
section
addition

## Materials

egg carton
permanent marker
two small items such as beans, buttons, pennies

## What to do

1. Using a permanent marker, place one to five dots in each of the sections of an egg carton. Put two beans, buttons, pennies or other small item in the bottom of the carton.
2. Close the lid and shake the carton. Then open the lid and have the children count the dots together in the sections where the two beans have landed.

★ THE INSTANT CURRICULUM

math activities

# Music and Movement Activities

## Circle Songs

**3+**

*This activity develops children's concentration.*

### Words to use

sing
move
circle
around

### Materials

### What to do

1. While singing a favorite song, the children make a circle and move in a circular fashion around the room.
2. A variation would be two circles of children, one smaller circle inside a larger circle.
3. A further variation would be several smaller circles of four to five children all singing and moving at the same time.

★ THE INSTANT CURRICULUM

## Divided Singing

**3+**

*Children practice listening skills and cooperation.*

### Words to use

my turn
your turn
everyone
verse
group
first
second
third

## Materials

## What to do

To vary a singing activity and to give children extended opportunities to learn new words, let various parts of the group sing the same verse.

*First time: All sing the verse.*
*Second time: Children sitting in chairs sing.*
*Third time: Children sitting on the floor sing.*

or

*First time: Boys sing.*
*Second time: Girls sing.*
*Third time: All sing.*

★ THE INSTANT CURRICULUM

# Preschool Fitness                                      3+

*This activity develops coordination and large muscle skills.*

## Words to use

| | |
|---|---|
| march | reach |
| flap | bow |
| curtsy | extend |
| stretch | move |
| dance | exercise |
| muscles | strong |
| healthy | |

## Materials

record of lively music

## What to do

Put on a lively record and have children do a variety of large muscle exercises. Examples: While marching to music, "reach for the stars," "flap your wings," or march "like toy soldiers." While standing in a circle, bow, curtsy, touch shoulders or extend arms.

★ THE INSTANT CURRICULUM

# One Elephant

*This activity develops children's coordination and large muscle development.*

## Words to use

elephant
trunk
tail
hold on

## Materials

## What to do

1. Sit in a circle. Select one child. She places one arm out in front to make a trunk and walks around the circle while the group sings the "One Elephant" song.
2. After singing, "She had such enormous fun, she called for another elephant to come," the first child chooses a second child.
3. Now the two children walk around the group. The first child continues to put one arm out front for a trunk. She also extends her other arm between her legs for a tail to hold the hand of the second child behind her. This second child is holding one arm in front for a trunk. This arm holds onto the arm of the first child (tail of the first elephant) that she is extending between her legs.
4. Continue with "Two elephants went out to play..." and so on.

★ WHERE IS THUMBKIN?

# Spider Dance

3+

*This activity encourages the children's creative expression.*

## Words to use

spider
crawl
legs
reach out

music & movement activities

## Materials

recordings of various types of music

## What to do

1. Play music and encourage the children to dance like spiders.
2. After a while, change to a different piece of music and ask the children to dance like spiders to it.

★ WHERE IS THUMBKIN?

# Dance a Garden                                          3+

*Creative movement and guided imagery are recognized methods for introducing or reviewing concepts—lots of us remember pretending to grow from acorns to oak trees in our early years. By using a bit of fruit as the initial food source, a plant mister to make it rain and the light switch to turn on the "sun," anyone can start a whole grove of oak trees, a bean patch or a daisy field. Children also get the chance to roll their tongues around the word photosynthesis, a word they like just as well as brontosaurus.*

## Words to use

| | |
|---|---|
| seeds | plant |
| grow | nutrients |
| shape | slow motion |
| photosynthesis | rain |
| sun | |

## Materials

record or tape player
quiet music "to grow by" (for example—"Sunshine on My Shoulders" or Beethoven's Pastoral Symphony)
plant mister with water
an assortment of seeds
enough fruit for each child to have a small piece (seedless grapes are easy)

## What to do

1. Show the children the collection of seeds and talk about how they grow into plants. Did anyone ever plant a garden? What do seeds need to grow? (Water and warmth to sprout, sunlight to continue to grow.) Tell them that all seeds, no matter what size or shape, have a little bit of food inside them to help the plant start to grow. Once the plant is in the sunlight, it can make most of its own food through photosynthesis. You may want to chant the word with the children a few times. Most of them will enjoy trying such a long word, especially said rhythmically.
2. Ask the children to become seeds, forming the tiniest body shapes they can create. What kind of seed are you? What plant will you become?
3. Turn off the lights. The seeds are under the ground in the dark. Start the music. Tell the children that they will begin to grow in slow motion when they have food and water.
4. Give each child a piece of fruit, but tell them they can't begin to eat until it rains. Using the plant mister, create rain for each child. They can then begin to sprout and eat the food stored in the seed. Encourage them to grow "in slow motion" just a little bit at a time.

5. Turn on the lights. Now the seedlings don't need their stored food anymore. They soak up the sunlight and make their own food through photosynthesis. Oh, but they're looking a little droopy. They can't make their own water. How about a little more rain?
6. When the "plants" are grown, ask them what they are. Discuss what would happen with no rain or sunlight.
7. Discuss what people need to grow.

**Want to do more?**

Grow seeds with and without water. Try peas, mung beans, radishes, or alfalfa for quick growth. Expose some to light and cover others. What happens? Discuss the importance of soil as a source of water and nutrients. Grow seeds with and without soil.

★ MUDPIES TO MAGNETS

# Gardening                                                    3+

*Children learn to pantomime the actions of gardening.*

## Words to use

gardening          digging
pantomime          move
no talking         silent
guess              act out

## Materials

## What to do

1. During group time, pantomime gardening down on your knees, digging in the dirt. Wipe your brow with the back of your hand or pretend to take a handkerchief from your pocket. Have the children guess what you are doing.
2. Let volunteers pantomime different actions. First, have the child whisper in your ear what action she is going to pantomime. Have her do it for the children so that they can guess what her motions mean.
3. Ask pairs of children to do some actions together for the group to guess.

## Teaching tips

Having the child whisper in your ear allows you to be able to assist her if she can't think of what to do. If the child freezes, you can say, "Would you like me to do it with you?" Then the child can imitate you. Younger children may need props to pantomime or may need to rehearse their movements in front of a mirror before doing them for the entire group.

★ MORE STORY S-T-R-E-T-C-H-E-R-S

# Science Activities

## Listening for Birds                                      3+

*Children learn to listen for sounds of birds.*

### Words to use

listen                  bird
chirp                   song

### Materials

cassette tape and recorder

### What to do

1. Have the children sit quietly on the edge of the playground near some trees and listen for at least three minutes without saying a word. Ask them what they hear—crickets, traffic and birds chirping and singing.
2. Sit quietly again for three to five minutes and have the children concentrate on the bird sounds.
3. Tape record the sounds from your outside quiet time.
4. Whisper an introduction to the tape telling where, when and why the tape was made.
5. Place the finished tape on the display table in the science and nature center.

### Teaching tips

Take a quiet walk in a nearby woods and listen for more bird sounds. Older children can take turns taking the tape recorder home to record nature sounds near their homes.

★ MORE STORY S-T-R-E-T-C-H-E-R-S

## Bird's Nest                                               3+

*Encourages the development of observation skills.*

### Words to use

bird                    materials
nest                    weave
examine                 mud
build                   beak

## Materials

a real bird's nest or several pictures of bird's nests and birds building nests
magnifying glass

## What to do

1. Invite the children to examine the bird's nest.
2. Call attention to the different types of materials used to build the nest.

★ Where Is Thumbkin?

# Dirt Day                                3+

*Children develop observation skills while learning about what things are found in dirt.*

## Words to use

| | |
|---|---|
| dirt | shovel |
| dig | observe |
| find | magnify |

## Materials

shovels
spade
spoons
water table or individual plastic tubs
sand, gravel, topsoil and clay-based dirt
magnifying glasses
paper cups
water
poster or paper
marker

## What to do

1. Announce the date of Dirt Day with a big poster. Request that children wear old play clothes and bring extra clothes to have on hand.
2. Empty the water table or set out several plastic tubs. Put out separate containers of sand, gravel, topsoil and clay-based dirt.
3. Label a paper cup for each child.
4. Make books and field guides about rocks and minerals available.
5. Take the children outside with shovels, spoons and a garden spade. Choose a spot and dig up a large spadeful to bring back to the classroom. Allow the children to explore the hole with their digging tools.
6. Bring a shovelful of dirt inside and place it in the empty water table (or in a few plastic tubs). Let the children comb through the dirt.

7. Record comments and observations on a large poster or individual work sheets. Ask, "Are there any living creatures? Rocks or stones? Any surprises (nails, glass, bones, etc.)?" If earthworms or insects are found, encourage gentle observation for a short period of time. Discuss their role in the environment, then bring a few children along to release the creatures outside.

8. Rocks, stones or pebbles discovered in the course of observation can be assembled in the science center as the beginning of a rock collection. Ask for other contributions.

9. Allow children to add water to the dirt and observe changes.

## Want to do more?

Make bricks by packing mud into the bottom half of cut-off wax milk cartons. Allow to dry in the sun and carefully peel off cartons. Talk about adobe houses.

## Books to read

*A Hole Is to Dig* by Ruth Krauss
*How to Dig a Hole to the Other Side of the Earth* by Faith McNulty

★ THE GIANT ENCYCLOPEDIA OF THEME ACTIVITIES

# The House of Worms                                3+

*Earthworms live in burrows in the soil and do not like daylight or robins. We can find them more easily at night in our backyards by using a flashlight and a fast hand. If we look for them during the day, we must be prepared to dig in the soil with a shovel. You can always buy earthworms in a bait shop.*

## Words to use

| | |
|---|---|
| worm | bristles |
| legs | move |
| burrow | food |
| home | house |

## Materials

soil
a tall narrow olive or pickle jar
water
earthworms
black paper
rubber bands
small bits of grass
leaves
lettuce
coffee grounds

## What to do

1. Collect some earthworms.
2. Collect enough soil to fill the narrow jar.
3. Fill the jar with damp soil—be sure it's not too wet as this will drown the worms.
4. Place the worms in the soil.
5. Put bits of food (lettuce, grass, leaves, coffee grounds) into the jar on top of the soil.
6. Wrap the jar with black paper and secure with two rubber bands.
7. Remove the paper the next day to see how the worms have burrowed along the glass. Did they eat any food?
8. Keep for several days. Can you discover their favorite food?
9. Release the worms in a safe place. Check in a while. How long does it take for them to burrow back into the ground?

## Want to do more?

Discuss the food that worms live on. They live on organic matter (things that were once alive) like dead animals, insect parts, dead leaves and plants. Hold a worm and watch how it moves. Try moving like worms.

★ MORE MUDPIES TO MAGNETS

# A House for Snugs (Short for Snails and Slugs)          3+

*Snails and slugs can make nice pets if we create a home that has perfect living conditions and an adequate food supply. This activity lets the children create a home for these pets. It also allows them to study the animals' unique characteristics, their movements and food preferences.*

## Words to use

slugs
snails
shell
movement
living conditions

## Materials

large clear container such as an aquarium or large jar
a number of small sheets of clear Plexiglas
slugs and snails collected from outside
rocks
sticks
grass
leaves
water

## What to do

1. Put an inch or so of soil in the bottom of the container. Add some rocks, sticks, leaves and grass. Add a small amount of water. It should be damp, not wet.
2. Collect snugs and place them in the snug house.
3. If you have fixed the snug house so that it is snug perfect, then the critters will come out and crawl around. Some will climb the glass and be observed. Now is the time for your children to study them.
4. Place an active snail or slug on a piece of clear Plexiglas. Wait for it to crawl. Pick up the Plexiglas and observe the snail or slug as it moves about. Observe from above and below.
5. Ask the children to describe what the movement looks like. Compare one snail's movement to another. Compare snails and slugs.

## Want to do more?

Use a crayon to draw the snail's path. Put a cup of warm water under the plate. What does the snail do? Try to see what snails or slugs like by putting different foods in their house. Can the children move to slow music like snails and slugs? Can they curl their bodies like a snail shell? Bring in other shells to examine.

★ More Mudpies to Magnets

# Egg Carton Gardens    3+

*Children learn observation skills and measurement concepts.*

## Words to use

seeds          grow
measure        growth
record         ruler

## Materials

egg carton (bottom only)
potting soil
marigold seeds
popsicle sticks
marker
ruler

## What to do

1. With the children, plant marigold seeds in an egg carton. Place potting soil in each crate of the carton. Then plant the seeds.
2. Put an unmarked popsicle stick in each crate to use as a measuring stick.
3. The children can use a marker to record weekly growth.
4. After several weeks, remove the popsicle stick and use a standard ruler to measure weekly growth.

★ Where Is Thumbkin?

# Plant Life

## 3+

*In this activity children are given the responsibility of planting a seed and caring for the plant that sprouts over a period of time. They may need to be reminded every day of their responsibility to care for the growing plant. Consider posting a list of duties with all their names that they can check off after completing tasks.*

## Words to use

life
grow
gentle
care
germinate
responsible
take care of
job
task

## Materials

enough seeds for all the children (use dill, chive, marigold or other seeds that germinate quickly)
a container filled with dirt for each child
marker

## What to do

1. Take the seeds out of the package and show them to the children. Talk about seeds and discuss how they grow when put into dirt and watered.
2. Place the containers on the table. Ask the children to plant their seeds. Label the containers with the children's names and place them in a sunny spot.
3. Water and care for the plants. A check-off chart listing necessary care and the children's names is helpful.
4. Talk with the children about the care that seeds need to help them grow. Extend the discussion to the care babies and young children need to grow to healthy adulthood.

## Want to do more?

Let children take the plants home after they begin to germinate and grow. Ask the children to keep their plants with them for a period of time. If they take them outside, for example, they should find a safe place for the plants while they play. Depending on the season, children can replant their plant outside in a small school garden. Responsibility for watering and weeding can be divided among the children.

## Home connection

Encourage parents and children to grow their own windowsill herb garden of chives.

★ THE PEACEFUL CLASSROOM

# Wheelbarrow or Wagon Gardens

**3+**

*This type of garden allows you to move the plants during the day to follow the sunshine. It is ideal for a playground with too much shade for successful gardening. The children learn about the importance of sun for the growth of plants.*

## Words to use

wheelbarrow
move
wheels
round
handles
push

## Materials

wheelbarrow or large
   wagon
plastic garbage bags
potting soil
gravel
small plants, such as
   petunias, marigolds or
   pansies

## What to do

1. First, line the wheelbarrow or wagon with a plastic garbage bag so that watering doesn't cause it to rust.
2. Put some gravel in next to provide drainage.
3. Fill with soil and plant the flowers.
4. Let the children help move the wheelbarrow to sunny spots during the day and water the plants.

★ THE OUTSIDE PLAY AND LEARNING BOOK

# Window Garden

**3+**

*Children learn to care for their own plants.*

## Words to use

windowsill           sun
shade               light
dark                grow
water              eyedropper

## Materials

empty milk cartons, cups or clay pots
potting soil
small plants
eyedropper

## What to do

1. Let the children plant small plants in empty milk cartons, cups or clay pots.
2. Discuss placement of the plants in a sunny vs. shady area.
3. Keep eyedroppers and a bowl of water nearby so that the children can water (but not overwater) their own plant every day.

★ THE INSTANT CURRICULUM

# Make a Rainbow                                              3+

*Teaches children about light reflection.*

## Words to use

reflect
reflection
mirror
angle
through
rainbow
beam
sunlight
shine
clear

## Materials

large, deep clear dish or glass
water
mirror

## What to do

1. Fill a large, deep clear dish or glass with water.
2. Be sure the water is motionless.
3. Put a mirror into the water at an angle so that sunlight goes through the water and reflects off the mirror.
4. Look at the wall where the mirror has projected a beam of sunlight making a rainbow!

★ 500 FIVE MINUTE GAMES

# Rainbow in a Jar 3+

*In this activity, the children watch colors float through water in beautiful designs and also see primary colors blend to create secondary colors. Peaceful music helps set the mood for calm relaxation.*

## Words to use

patterns
diffusion
mix
blend
rainbow
colors
shapes
currents
experiment
compare

## Materials

1 gallon glass jar
food coloring
tape or record player
"Rainbow Connection" or similar song on tape or record
water

## What to do

1. Fill a gallon glass jar with water and place the jar where the children can observe it from all sides. This works best if the water sits overnight so that the currents from the top can subside. Diffusion will then occur at a slow, natural pace.
2. Play the song "Rainbow Connection" or a song of your choice on a tape or record player.
3. Place one drop of the primary colors (red, yellow, blue) in the jar. Dropping the colors in from a height of two to three inches will cause the color streams to go deeper.
4. Observe the colors as they slowly spread through the water, forming interesting shapes and patterns as they blend into the colors of a rainbow.
Note: This is not a time for teacher talk. Give the children a chance to reflect quietly as the music plays.

## Want to do more?

Experiment with a variety of color mixtures to discover how colors blend to create new colors. Use one jar of quiet water and one freshly filled jar. Compare diffusion patterns. Try hot water or sugar water. Use small jars and let the children do it themselves. Drop the colors in from different heights. What happens when you use tempera paint or ink? Give the children colored scarves and let them move and dance to the music as the colors are moving in the jar.

★ Mudpies to Magnets

# Changing Colors

**3+**

*What would the world look like if everything was green? Find out with this activity.*

### Words to use

color words
cellophane
objects

### Materials

four shoe boxes
scissors
tape
cellophane paper in four
  colors
items from the class-
  room

*Cut a large circular opening at the top of each lid*

*tape 4 different colors of cellophane on bottom side of lid under circular opening*

### What to do

1. Find four shoe boxes of the same size with interchangeable lids.
2. Cut a large circular opening in the top of each lid.
3. Tape a piece of cellophane paper on the bottom side of the lid making sure that each box has a different color.
4. Collect familiar objects that will fit inside of the shoe boxes so the children can see how they look in different colors. Possible items for viewing include a wooden block, a doll, a plastic fork, a piece of paper, a white mug, an envelope and a small plastic bottle.

★ THE COMPLETE LEARNING CENTER BOOK

# Puddle Walk

**4+**

*This activity uses the puddle as a teaching tool to help children predict the possible presence of a future puddle. It also checks the "puddleability" of the area so that the next time it rains, the class can take a "puddle walk" to see if puddles form.*

### Words to use

evaporation            puddles
measure                depth
circumference          rain
diameter               record

## Materials

meter stick or yardstick•
paper or crayons for recording purposes

## What to do

1. After a rain storm, take a puddle walk. Ask the children to see how many puddles they can find.
2. Record the characteristics of the puddles.
   - ✓ a. circumference—How big around are they?
   - ✓ b. depth—How deep are they? (Use a measuring stick.)
   - ✓ c. diameter—To measure the puddle's diameter, walk through it, lay a stick across it or stretch string across it.
   - ✓ d. Where do puddles usually form?
3. Return to observe the puddles the next day. What changes are there from the characteristics recorded on the first day? Repeat step 2. Are the puddles bigger or smaller? What do you think causes some puddles to last longer than others?

## Want to do more?

Predict where puddles will be formed before the next rainstorm. Fill soda bottles with water so you start with equal amounts of water. Let the children make their own puddles. Then predict which will evaporate first, which will last the longest and which will be the deepest.

★ MUDPIES TO MAGNETS

# Seed Power                                                    4+

*Geologists state that soil is formed by the roots of plants that break down rocks by slow, steady pressure. Wind and water also affect rock, forming soil, but this is a very slow process and is difficult to show to children. Seed Power serves to demonstrate on a small scale just how powerful the simple sprouting of a seed can be.*

## Words to use

plant
growth
smother
prevent
surfaces
seeds
germinate
sprout
power
strong
strength

fill with soil

fill with soil
and plaster of paris
on top

## Materials

plaster of Paris            small clear plastic containers
water                       lima bean seeds
potting soil

## What to do

1. Fill two clear plastic containers half full of potting soil or sand.
2. Plant three lima bean seeds in one container.
3. Water until moist, but not soaked.
4. Place three lima beans on top of the soil in the second container.
5. Mix plaster of Paris and water. Make it runny.
6. Pour a thin layer of plaster of Paris over the beans in the second container. Use just enough to cover the seeds.
7. The seeds must be kept moist. Water them every day.
8. How do you think this plaster of Paris cover will affect the growth of the seeds? Will it smother them or do you think they will grow? Record the children's predictions.
9. Observe the containers for two weeks and compare. What happens to the seeds? What do you think happens to plants that are covered by blacktop or concrete to make surfaces for parking lots and playgrounds?

## Want to do more?

Try other seeds. Are some stronger than others? Take a walk and look for things growing through cracks.

★ MUDPIES TO MAGNETS

# Scientific Observations                          4+

*Encourages the development of visual discrimination.*

## Words to use

photograph          spider
insects             differences
similarities        legs

## Materials

spider and insect  photos

## What to do

1. Display photographs of spiders in the science center along with photographs of other insects.
2. Encourage the children to look for differences and similarities between spiders and other insects.

★ WHERE IS THUMBKIN?

# Raindrop Close-ups

**5+**

*Teaches children observation skills.*

## Words to use

magnify
magnifying glass
drop
examine

## Materials

eyedroppers
container of water
plate
magnifying glass

## What to do

1. The children use the eyedropper to place a drop of water on the plate.
2. Then they use the magnifying glass to look closely at the water.
3. Talk about the way the water holds its shape. Explain that water has a protective "skin."
4. Have the children touch the drop of water, thus breaking the "skin." What happens?

★ WHERE IS THUMBKIN?


# Simple Sundial

**5+**

*Older children may get a stronger sense of the length of an hour, as well as the relationship between the position of the sun and the time of day. Younger children may become more conscious of the sequence of events in the day.*

## Words to use

sun
sundial
shadow

## Materials

a stick
sunny spot

## What to do

1. Put the stick into the ground so it is completely vertical and in a sunny spot.
2. The first day, mark the spot on the ground where the shadow of the stick ends each hour on the hour.

3. On the second day, you will be able to tell time accurately using the sundial, providing the stick has remained stable and the sun is shining.

4. This activity is most appropriate for older children.

## Want to do more?

For younger children, you could note "event time" instead of "clock time." Time for morning snack, time to go outside, time to go inside and lunch time are events that could be noted on your dial.

★ THE OUTSIDE PLAY AND LEARNING BOOK

# Snack and Cooking Activities

## Tasty Treats

**3+**

*Children love to prepare their own snacks.*

### Words to use

measure
mix
add
spoonsful

### Materials

butterscotch chips
chow mein noodles
peanuts
spoon
wax paper

1 small package
butterscotch chips

1 small can chow
mein noodles

1 can peanuts

1 tsp. water

Heat chips over hot water.

Fold in noodles.

Add peanuts.

Add water as needed.

Drop by rounded spoonfuls onto waxed paper
cookie sheet

Chill 30 mins.

## What to do

1. Let the children prepare recipes that have an unusual combination of ingredients or taste variations.
2. Use recipe cards or charts that allow the children to work alone or in small groups. Interesting snacks include the following:

### Trail Mix

Children choose the ingredients to combine into a trail mix in ziplock bags. Suggestions for ingredients include nuts, marshmallows, pretzels, raisins, chocolate chips, Chinese noodles, goldfish crackers, dry cereal.

### Fruity Art

Use fruit and other edible items to create edible art on aluminum pie pans or Styrofoam meat trays. Suggestions include apple slices, cherries, cheese, oranges, bananas, raisins, marshmallows, grapes, kiwi, olive.

★ THE COMPLETE LEARNING CENTER BOOK

# Green Snacks                    3+

*A tasty and fun way to learn about colors.*

## Words to use

color words
taste
compare
sweet
sour
salty
crunchy
tastes good

## Materials

green gelatin
green grapes
celery
green olives
broccoli
bowls

## What to do

1. Make the gelatin with the children's help.
2. When the gelatin is ready to serve, add grapes, olives, celery and broccoli to the menu.
3. The children taste the various green items and make comparisons.

★ WHERE IS THUMBKIN?

# Gelatin Rainbows

**3+**

*Children learn about colors and how to prepare a snack.*

## Words to use

rainbow          layers
colors           on top of
gelatin          rainbow

## Materials

three or four flavored gelatins
large glass dish
bowls
spoons

## What to do

1. Prepare one gelatin at a time. Let it cool and set before preparing the next.
2. Layer gelatins to create a rainbow effect.
3. Serve, eat and enjoy!

★ WHERE IS THUMBKIN?

# Harold's Purple Fruits

**3+**

*Children learn to associate purple with a color that appears in natural foods.*

## Words to use

purple
plum
prune
grapes
taste

## Materials

*Harold and the Purple Crayon* by Crockett Johnson
plums
seedless prunes
purple seedless grapes for eating
prunes and grapes with seeds for demonstration
knife
scissors
purple construction paper
napkins

## What to do

1. On a day when you read *Harold and the Purple Crayon,* place seedless grapes, seedless prunes and plums in a nice arrangement on the snack tables.
2. Let the children use the scissors to snip off a little bunch of grapes.
3. Call attention to the fact that the purple grapes are seedless.
4. Ask the children to guess whether or not there are seeds in the plums and prunes.
5. Have them eat a plum and leave the seed on their napkin.
6. Ask them to guess whether or not there is a seed in the prune, then eat the prune to decide.
7. Cut open a seedless grape and a grape with seeds and show them the difference.
8. Cut open a seedless prune and a prune with seeds and show them the difference.
9. Discuss that prunes are dried plums.

## Teaching tips

Whenever possible, emphasize healthy natural snacks. Also, do not force any child to eat something she or he does not want.

★ MORE STORY S-T-R-E-T-C-H-E-R-S

# Picnic on a Lovely Spring Day                                3+

*Children learn to plan and prepare their snack to be served outside.*

## Words to use

picnic
picnic basket
outside

## Materials

cheese
crackers
variety of fruits
plastic knives
peanut butter
juice or milk
napkins
tablecloths
picnic basket

## What to do

1. Ask the children to plan some simple foods they might prepare for a snack to take on a picnic. Possibilities include cheese and crackers, fruit and peanut butter and crackers.
2. Let the snack helpers pack the picnic snack in a picnic basket.
3. Once outside, let other helpers prepare cheese and crackers, peanut butter and crackers and sliced fruit.

4. Ask other children to help by setting out napkins and fruit juice or milk.
5. A clean-up crew can dispose of the paper napkins, fold tablecloths and wash plastic knives for reuse.

## Teaching tips

Let the children sit on the ground if it is warm and dry. Enjoy their company and conversation in a leisurely manner without rushing on to other activities. Picnics are for lounging around and savoring the beauty of nature.

★ MORE STORY S-t-r-e-t-c-h-e-r-s

# Carrot and Raisin Salad                    3+

*Children learn to prepare a nutritious snack.*

## Words to use

wash
carrots
salad
peel

## Materials

carrots, one per child
raisins
vegetable peelers
paper towels
bowls

## What to do

1. Ask some children to help wash the carrots.
2. Demonstrate how to hold the carrot and use the vegetable peeler to make slivers of carrots.
3. Let each child take a carrot and use the vegetable peeler to make a mound of carrot slivers.
4. Place the shredded carrots into a bowl and sprinkle in the raisins.
5. Place the carrot and raisin salad in the refrigerator to chill. Serve at snack time.

## Teaching tips

If the carrot and raisin salad is not moist enough, add a teaspoon of French dressing to the salad; however, we find most children enjoy the salad without the dressing. Also, vary the recipe by adding chopped apples or nuts. Make different recipes and let the children decide which they like best.

★ STORY S-t-r-e-t-c-h-e-r-s

snack & cooking activities

## Make Rain

**3+**

*The sound of rain brings peace to the classroom. Children are enchanted by making the sound of rain, which calms them down and enables them to follow directions.*

### Words to use

rain
gentle
calm

### Materials

### What to do

1. Ask the children to help make rain.
2. Tell them they just need to watch you and do what you do.
3. Make each of the sounds below for five or ten seconds.

> *Slide palms back and forth.*
> *Tap fingers together.*
> *Snap fingers.*
> *Clap hands.*
> *Slap thighs.*
> *Stomp feet.*
> *Slap thighs.*
> *Clap hands.*
> *Snap fingers.*
> *Tap fingers together.*
> *Slide your palms back and forth.*
> *Lay your hands quietly in your lap.*

### Want to do more?

Make rain in a round. Divide the class into two groups. Have one side begin a motion, then bring in the other side a few seconds later. Continue working through all the motions. This works well if there is an adult to lead each group.

★ TRANSITION TIME

# Baby Birds

**3+**

*Use this activity to lower the noise level in the room or keep children occupied while waiting to begin a new activity. Children need to use auditory discrimination skills to find their Baby Birds.*

## Words to use

bird
mama
papa
baby
listen
chirp

## Materials

## What to do

1. Children sit on the floor or in chairs.
2. One child is selected to be "mama bird" or "papa bird" and leaves the room.
3. While this child is out of the room, five other children are chosen to be baby birds.
4. All the children put their heads down and the mama or papa bird is called back into the room.
5. The baby birds begin "chirping" as mama or papa goes around and tries to identify who they are.
6. When all the baby birds have been found, begin another round of the game.

## Want to do more?

Use different animals to play this game. Pretend to be puppies, kittens, cubs, etc.

★ TRANSITION TIME

# Twiddle Your Thumbs

**3+**

*This is a great transition fingerplay to helps children quiet down.*

## Words to use

| | |
|---|---|
| twiddle | thumb |
| clap | stamp |
| bridge | arch |
| hands | poem |

## Materials

## What to do

Recite the poem and carry out the actions.

> *You twiddle your thumbs,*
> *And clap your hands,*
> *And then you stamp your feet.*
>
> *You turn to the left,*
> *You turn to the right,*
> *And make your fingers meet.*
>
> *You make a bridge,*
> *You make an arch,*
> *You give another clap.*
>
> *You wave your hands,*
> *You fold your hands,*
> *And put them in your lap.*

★ 500 FIVE MINUTE GAMES

# Partner Moves

3+

*This is a good transition activity that also promotes social skills.*

## Words to use

partner
cooperate
forward
backward
scoot
swim
skip

## Materials

## What to do

1. Ask the children to think of ways to move to another part of the room with a friend. A few possibilities include:

*Holding hands facing forward.*
*Holding hands facing backward.*
*Holding hands with one forward and one backward.*
*Sitting on the floor scooting.*
*Lying on the floor swimming.*
*Hopping, jumping or skipping.*

★ 500 Five Minute Games

# Transition Time                    3+

*Some children like a little private time when they arrive in the morning, while other children need to be alone at other times during the day. There is very little privacy for children in most school environments, so it's important to have a place where they can get away from the group and be alone.*

## Words to use

private                    privacy
alone                      relax

## Materials

appliance box or other large box
sharp knife
markers or paints
pillows, soft animals and books

## What to do

1. Cut a door and windows in the box with a sharp knife. (An adult will need to do this.)
2. Let the children decorate the box with paints or markers.
3. Place the box in a quiet area of the room and fill with pillows, soft animals and books.
4. Discuss different feelings with the children and tell them that you understand that sometimes they want to be with other people, but sometimes they just want to be by themselves.
5. Tell the children that when they want to be alone, they can go to the Cozy Corner to think, read a book, dream or relax. (Limit the number of children who can use this space at the same time to one or two.)

## Want to do more?

Use old blankets, sheets or scarves to create a "dream center." Hang stars inside and fill with pillows or large beanbags. Create a private space by pulling a bookshelf away from a wall, or filling a large plastic cube with pillows and blankets. Add a listening center with some peaceful music or environmental sounds to the Cozy Corner.

★ Transition Time

# Early Risers

*Children have different sleep needs. Those who do not nap or who wake early will enjoy these activities. Offer those who are awake the choice of an alternative quiet activity.*

## Words to use

quiet
play
rest
sleep
nap
read
puzzles
look at

## Materials

table toys (puzzles, beads, pegboard, etc.)
listening station (tapes and books)
open-ended art materials (markers, collage materials, scissors, etc.)
books and magazines

## What to do

1. After children have been given ample opportunity to sleep or rest (state licensing standards may specify this), ask them softly if they would like to go to the quiet table to work with one of the materials listed above.

## Want to do more?

Let one teacher take the children who wake early into another room to play games or do activities. Set out a self-serve snack for children who wake early. Prepare a nap time basket with lacing cards, playdough, blank books and markers and other quiet activities children can do on their cots.

★ TRANSITION TIME

APRIL

transition activities

# Games

## Puddle Game

**3+**

*This activity facilitates gross motor control and reinforces spatial concepts. It can be used as part of a unit on weather or on a rainy day.*

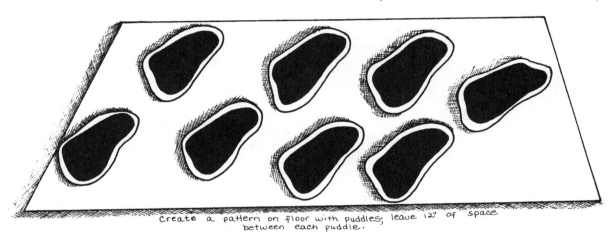

Create a pattern on floor with puddles; leave 12" of space between each puddle.

### Words to use

puddle pattern
jump over

### Materials

cardboard blue construction paper
scissors contact paper

### What to do

1. Make a puddle-shaped template from the cardboard, approximately 8" x 12" in size.
2. Trace and cut out eight to ten blue construction paper "puddles."
3. Cover the "puddles" with contact paper for durability.
4. For the activity, line up puddles in a pattern on the floor with 12" spaces between each puddle.
5. Have the children take turns jumping over the puddles.

### Want to do more?

You can combine the individual puddles to make larger ones to jump over. The children can pretend to be animals jumping in and out of the puddles.

★ THE GIANT ENCYCLOPEDIA OF THEME ACTIVITIES

# Balls

**3+**

*The exciting thing about balls is that they are great cause and effect toys. The person creates the cause—the action on the ball—and the ball produces the effect by moving in different ways. Change the cause, and the effect changes. The variations are endless and always fascinating. Here are a few simple activities to get the children started.*

## Words to use

| | |
|---|---|
| ball | roll |
| slide | catch |
| circle | knock over |
| beach ball | throw |
| target | |

## Materials

assorted balls
milk carton
cardboard box
sharp knife (for teachers)
juice cans

## What to do

### Rolling Games

1. Roll the ball down the slide and let a child at the bottom catch it.
2. Roll the ball against a wall and let a child retrieve it on its way back.
3. Have the children sit or stand in a circle. Place an object, such as a milk carton, in the middle of the circle. Let the children roll the ball to try to knock over the object. Create a greater challenge by providing a smaller ball or making a larger circle.

### Catching Games

1. Start with a large ball, like a beach ball. The young children will catch first with their whole body. Later they will use their forearms and finally just their hands.
2. Stand a few feet away from the child and throw a light ball. Let the child throw it back to you. Increasing the distance or changing to smaller balls makes this more difficult.
3. Throw a ball to a child standing about ten feet away, making the ball bounce once in between.
4. Let the child bounce the ball on the ground so it goes against a wall and back out, then the child catches the ball on the return.

### Throwing Games

1. Throw a ball at a target. A basketball net, mounted low, is a popular item on many playgrounds, and there are commercial variations for young children that are adjustable and moveable.
2. You could make a target from a cardboard barrel or a tall box. Cut a round "mouth" hole, larger than a ball, at the bottom. Fit a piece of cardboard or board inside the barrel so the ball rolls out again.
3. For older children, make a "target throw" game, similar to ones found at carnivals. Line up several juice cans or other unbreakable targets on a board. Each could be given a point value. Let the children decide where to draw the throwing line. Each child could be given three chances to knock over the cans. Scores could be added up.

**Kicking Games**

1. Just kicking a ball is a complex accomplishment for a toddler or two year-old. They have to balance on one foot while swinging the other leg.
2. As the children gain skill in kicking a ball, see if they can kick it at a large target, such as a section of the fence. Later you can challenge the children to kick the ball, soccer style, all around the playground or on a course you map out.

★ THE OUTSIDE PLAY AND LEARNING BOOK

# Books

*Anansi the Spider: A Tale from the Ashanti* by Gerald McDermott
*Aranea: A Story about a Spider* by Jenny Wagner
*A Walk in the Rain* by Ursel Scheffler
*Be Nice to Spiders* by Margaret B. Graham
*Bringing the Rain to Kapiti Plain* by Verna Aardema
*The Giving Tree* by Shel Silverstein
*The Grass Is Always Greener* by Jez Alborough
*The Green Grass Grows All Around* by Hilde Hoffman
*Harold and the Purple Crayon* by Crockett Johnson
*A House of Leaves* by Kiyoshi Soya
*In My Treehouse* by Alice Schertle
*Listen to the Rain* by Bill Martin, Jr. and John Archambault
*The Little Engine That Could* by Watty Piper
*My Garden Grows* by Aldren Watson
*My Spring Robin* by Anne Rockwell
*Once There Was a Tree* by Natalia Romanova
*Over in the Meadow* by Olive A. Wadsworth
*Rain* by Peter Spiers
*Rain, Drop, Splash* by Alvin Tresselt
*Rain Talk* by Mary Serfozo
*The Reason for a Flower* by Ruth Heller
*Sarah's Questions* by Harriett Ziefert
*Sleepy Bear* by Lydia Dabcovich
*This Year's Garden* by Cynthia Rylant
*Thunder Cake* by Patricia Polacco
*Thunderstorm* by Mary Szilagyi
*A Tree Is Nice* by Janice Udry
*The Very Busy Spider* by Eric Carle
*A Walk in the Rain* by Ursel Scheffler
*What Is a Flower* by Jennifer W. Day

# Records, Tapes and CDs

Beall, Pamela Conn and Susan Hagen Nipp. "Eentsy Weentsy Spider" from *Wee Sing Children's Songs and Fingerplays*. Price Stern Sloan, 1979.

Beall, Pamela Conn and Susan Hagen Nipp. "The Green Grass Grows All Around" from *Wee Sing Silly Songs*. Price Stern Sloan.

Beall, Pamela Conn and Susan Hagen Nipp. "Over in the Meadow" from *Wee Sing Nursery Rhymes and Lullabies*. Price Stern Sloan.

Hammett, Carol and Elaine Bueffel "Itsy Bitsy Spider" from *It's Toddler Time*. Kimbo, 1982.

Moore, Thomas. "Itsy Bitsy Spider" from *Singing, Learning and Moving*. Thomas Moore Records.

Moore, Thomas. "The Frog Family" from *The Family*. Thomas Moore Records.

Weissman, Jackie. "Eensy Weensy Spider" from *Miss Jackie and Her Friends Sing About Peanut Butter, Tarzan and Roosters*. Miss Jackie, 1981.

Wisher, Tom and Teresa Whitaker. "How Does It Feel to Be a Fish" from *We've Got to Come Full Circle*. Folkways.

# Spring MAY

# Fingerplays, Poems and Songs

MAY

## One, Two, Buckle My Shoe

One, two, buckle my shoe
Three, four, shut the door
Five, six, pick up sticks
Seven, eight, lay them straight
Nine, ten, a good fat hen
Eleven, twelve, dig and delve
Thirteen, fourteen, maids a-courting
Fifteen, sixteen, maids a-milking
Seventeen, eighteen, maids a-waiting
Nineteen, twenty, my plate is empty.

★ ONE POTATO, TWO POTATO, THREE POTATO, FOUR

## There Were Five in the Bed

There were five in the bed and the little one
    said,
"Roll over. Roll over."
So they all rolled over and one fell out— (pause).
There were four in the bed and the little one
    said,
"Roll over. Roll over."
So they all rolled over and one fell out— (pause).
(Continue with numbers three and two.)
There was one in the bed and the little one said,
"GOOD NIGHT!"

★ ONE POTATO, TWO POTATO, THREE POTATO, FOUR

## One, Two, Three, Four

One, two, three, four,
Mary at the classroom door;
Five, six, seven, eight,
Eating cherries off her plate.

★ ONE POTATO, TWO POTATO, THREE POTATO, FOUR

## Ten Little Fingers

I have ten little fingers,
And they all belong to me.
I can make them do things.
Would you like to see?

I can shut them up tight
Or open them wide.
I can put them together
Or make them all hide.
I can make them jump high
Or make them go low.
I can fold them up quietly
And sit just so.

## The Beehive

Here is the beehive.
Where are the bees?
Hidden away where nobody sees.
Watch as they come out of their hive—
One, two, three, four, five!
They're alive!
BZZZ!

# Five Little Ducks

Five little ducks
Went out to play.
Over the hill and far away.
Mama Duck called with a
Quack-quack-quack,
Four little ducks came swimming back.

Four little ducks
Went out to play.
Over the hills and far away.
Mama Duck called with a
Quack-quack-quack,
Three little ducks came
Swimming back.

Three little ducks....
Two little ducks....

One little duck
Went out to play
Over the hill and far away,
Papa Duck called with a
Quack-quack-quack,
Five little ducks
Came swimming back!

With all their friends.

★ WHERE IS THUMBKIN?

# Six White Ducks

Six white ducks that I once knew
Fat ducks, skinny ducks, fair ones, too.
But the one little duck with a feather on his back
He ruled the others with a quack, quack, quack!
Quack, quack, quack, quack, quack, quack.
He ruled the others with a quack, quack, quack.

Down to the river they would go,
Wibble, wobble, wibble, wobble all in a row.
But the one little duck with a feather on his back
He ruled the others with a quack, quack, quack!
Quack, quack, quack, quack, quack, quack.
He led the others with a quack, quack, quack.

Home from the river they would come,
Wibble, wobble, wibble, wobble, ho-hum-hum!
But the one little duck with a feather on his back
He led the others with a quack, quack, quack!
Quack, quack, quack, quack, quack, quack.
He led the others with a quack, quack, quack.

★ WHERE IS THUMBKIN?

# Three Little Monkeys

Three little monkeys
Jumping on the bed,
One fell off and bumped his head,
Mother called the doctor and the doctor said,
"No more monkeys jumping on the bed."

Two little monkeys
Jumping on the bed,
One fell off and bumped his head,
Mother called the doctor and the doctor said,
"No more monkeys jumping on the bed."

One little monkey
Jumping on the bed,
One fell off and bumped his head,
Mother called the doctor and the doctor said,
"Get those monkeys back to bed."

★ WHERE IS THUMBKIN?

# The Ants Go Marching

The ants go marching one by one,
Hurrah, hurrah.
The ants go marching one by one,
Hurrah, hurrah.
The ants go marching one by one,
The little one stops to suck his thumb.
And they all go marching down
Into ground to get out of the rain,
BOOM! BOOM! BOOM!

Two...tie his shoe....
Three...climb a tree....
Four...shut the door....
Five...take a dive....
Six... pick up sticks....
Seven...pray to heaven....
Eight...shut the gate....
Nine...check the time....
Ten...say "THE END."

★ WHERE IS THUMBKIN?

# There Was an Old Lady

There was an old lady who swallowed a fly,
I don't know why she swallowed a fly,
Perhaps she'll die.

There was an old lady who swallowed a spider,
That wriggled and wriggled and tickled inside
    her;
She swallowed the spider to catch the fly,
I don't know why she swallowed the fly,
Perhaps she'll die.

There was an old lady who swallowed a bird,
Now, ain't it absurd to swallow a bird;
She swallowed a bird to catch the spider,
She swallowed the spider to catch the fly, etc.

There was an old lady who swallowed a cat,
Now fancy that, to swallow a cat, etc.

There was an old lady who swallowed a dog,
Oh, what a hog to swallow a dog, etc.

There was an old lady who swallowed a cow,
I don't know how she swallowed a cow, etc.

There was an old lady who swallowed a horse,
(Spoken) She died, of course!

★ WHERE IS THUMBKIN?

# One, Two, Three, Four, and Five

One, two, three, four, and five,
I caught a hare alive;
Six, seven, eight, nine, and ten,
I let him go again.

MAY

fingerplays, songs & poems

170

# Little Drops of Water

Little drops of water,
Little grains of sand,
Make the mighty ocean,
And the pleasant land.

# Little Jumping Joan

Here I am
Little Jumping Joan;
When nobody's with me
I'm always alone.

# If All the World

If all the world were apple pie,
And all the seas were ink,
And all the trees were bread and cheese
What should we have for drink?

# A Swarm of Bees

A swarm of bees in May
Is worth a load of hay;
A swarm of bees in June
Is worth a silver spoon;
A swarm of bees in July
Is not worth a fly.

# I'll tell You a Story

I'll tell you a story
About Jack a Nory,
And now my story's begun;
I'll tell you another
About Jack and his brother,
And now my story is done.

# Draw the Latch

Cross-patch
Draw the latch,
Sit by the fire and spin;
Take a cup and drink it up,
Then call your neighbors in.

# May Learning Centers

## Pet Center

### While children are playing in the Pet Center they:

1. Develop an understanding of responsibility as they care for and nurture pets (and pretend pets).
2. Enhance their interest in books as they listen to and "read" stories about pets.
3. Expand their oral language as they discuss pets.
4. Experience positive social interactions between each other through cooperative activities.

### Suggested props for the Pet Center

medium-size cardboard boxes (can be found at grocery stores or discount houses)
pet supplies such as
    brush
    comb
    blow dryer
empty labeled con-
    tainers such as
    flea powder
    hair conditioner
    shampoo
    dog food
    cat food
    bird food
    fish food, etc.
newspaper
bird cage
aquarium with fish
class pet (hamster,
    guinea pig or
    white mice)
stuffed animals that
    can be used as
    "pets" in the
    center

## Curriculum Connections

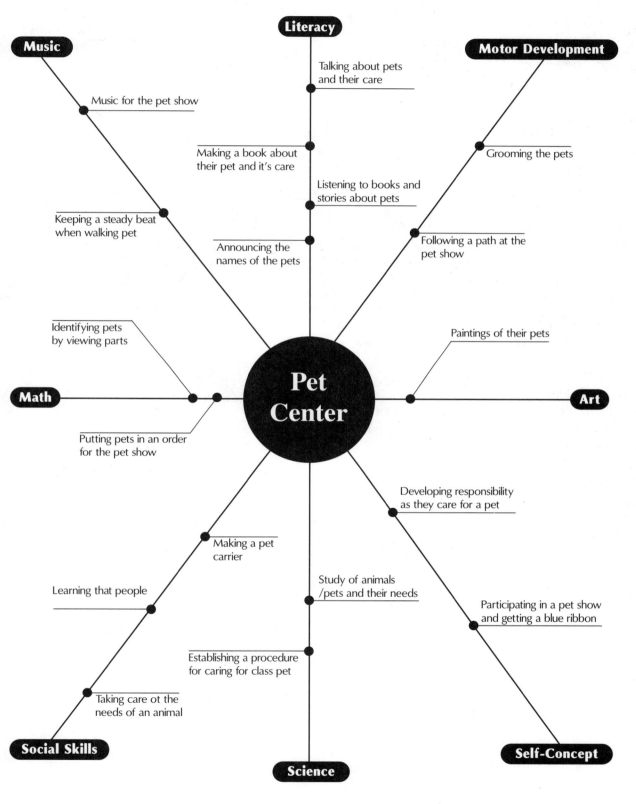

**Music**

Music for the pet show

Keeping a steady beat when walking pet

**Literacy**

Talking about pets and their care

Making a book about their pet and it's care

Listening to books and stories about pets

Announcing the names of the pets

**Motor Development**

Grooming the pets

Following a path at the pet show

**Math**

Identifying pets by viewing parts

Putting pets in an order for the pet show

**Pet Center**

Paintings of their pets

**Art**

Developing responsibility as they care for a pet

Making a pet carrier

Learning that people

Study of animals /pets and their needs

Participating in a pet show and getting a blue ribbon

Establishing a procedure for caring for class pet

Taking care ot the needs of an animal

**Social Skills**

**Science**

**Self-Concept**

★ THE COMPLETE LEARNING CENTER BOOK

# Party Center

**While children are playing in the Party Center they:**

1. Develop language skills as they communicate with others.
2. Enjoy listening to quality children's books and rereading them in the center.
3. Enhance their social skills as they cooperate and share at the party.
4. Use the themes and content of children's books in their play.

## Suggested props for the Party Center

*A Letter to Amy* by Ezra Jack Keats

*Birthday Presents* by Cynthia Rylant

*Clifford's Birthday Party* by Norman Bridwell

*The Birthday Thing* by SuAnn Kiser and Kevin Kiser

two low tables

plastic table cloths or sheets

small cardboard boxes

wrapping paper

bows

stickers and tags

tape

scissors

fancy dress-up clothes

## Curriculum Connections

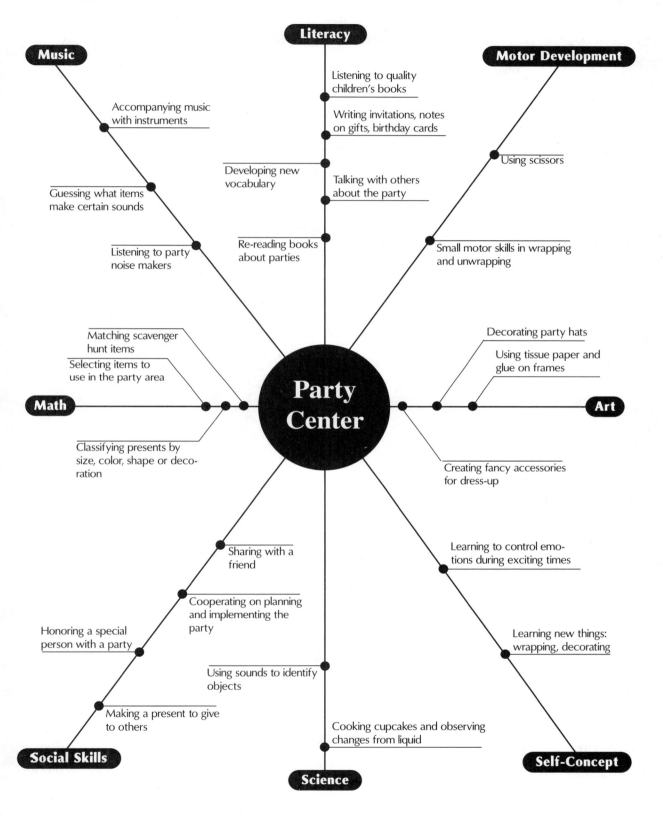

**Music**
- Accompanying music with instruments
- Guessing what items make certain sounds
- Listening to party noise makers

**Literacy**
- Listening to quality children's books
- Writing invitations, notes on gifts, birthday cards
- Developing new vocabulary
- Talking with others about the party
- Re-reading books about parties

**Motor Development**
- Using scissors
- Small motor skills in wrapping and unwrapping

**Math**
- Matching scavenger hunt items
- Selecting items to use in the party area
- Classifying presents by size, color, shape or decoration

**Art**
- Decorating party hats
- Using tissue paper and glue on frames
- Creating fancy accessories for dress-up

**Party Center**

**Social Skills**
- Sharing with a friend
- Cooperating on planning and implementing the party
- Honoring a special person with a party
- Making a present to give to others

**Science**
- Using sounds to identify objects
- Cooking cupcakes and observing changes from liquid

**Self-Concept**
- Learning to control emotions during exciting times
- Learning new things: wrapping, decorating

★ THE COMPLETE LEARNING CENTER BOOK

MAY

learning centers

# Art Activities

## Torn Paper Collage Animals

**3+**

*Children learn to make collages of scraps of construction paper.*

### Words to use

collage
animal
outline
fill in
little pieces
tear
torn

### Materials

*Rooster's Off to See the World* by Eric Carle
scraps of brightly colored construction paper
whole sheets of white and blue construction paper
crayons or markers
glue

cover animal outline with torn paper pieces

### What to do

1. Have the children select characters from the story and draw on a sheet of construction paper very large outlines of the one rooster, the two cats, the three frogs, the four turtles or the five fish. If they select the fish, they can draw five large fish on the blue construction paper.
2. Show the children Eric Carle's illustrations and how they are composed of many little pieces.
3. Demonstrate how to tear the construction paper scraps and glue them on. The children fill in the outlines with torn paper to make the collages.

### Teaching tips

For younger children, precut the shapes, and the children can tear the scraps of paper and glue them on. For older children, vary the activity by using colored tissue paper, or have them add dapples of paint onto their finished collages to create more texture, like Carle's illustrations.

★ More Story S-t-r-e-t-c-h-e-r-s

176

# Monkey Mask

3+

*What fun to pretend to be a monkey with this mask!*

## Words to use

monkey
face
nose
eyes
mouth

## Materials

paper plates
scissors
construction paper
crayons
stapler

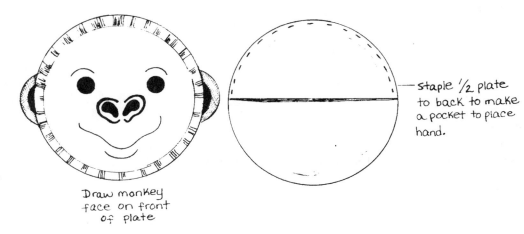

Draw monkey face on front of plate

staple ½ plate to back to make a pocket to place hand.

## What to do

1. Cut several paper plates in half and give each child a whole plate and a half plate.
2. The children design and color the whole plate to be the face of a monkey.
3. Staple the half plate onto the back of the whole plate to form a pocket for holding the mask.

★ WHERE IS THUMBKIN?

# Thumbprint Ants

3+

*Children learn about the parts of the body of an ant.*

## Words to use

thumbprint
legs
antennae
eyes

## Materials

ink pad
markers
paper

## What to do

Show the children how to create an ant by making three connected thumbprints and then using a marker to add details—six legs, antennae, etc.

★ WHERE IS THUMBKIN?

# Drawing in the Sand

**3+**

*Children learn that objects make surprising lines and patterns in the sand. They use their imagination as they use objects from nature to represent things such as eyes and hair in their drawings.*

## Words to use

draw                    lines
patterns                shapes
pictures

## Materials

sticks
sand combs
natural objects such as stones, pine cones or pine needles

## What to do

1. Encourage the children to make lines, shapes and designs in the sand using the sticks and other materials.
2. You might start by simply doing this yourself and see if the children pick up the idea.
3. Do not tell the children what to draw or make. Simply be interested in the pattern of lines and shapes that appears.
4. Older children may spontaneously draw faces or pictures of things.

## Want to do more?

Collect different materials on different days for the children to use. For instance, an assortment of stones and pebbles may inspire different uses than pine cones and pine needles.

★ THE OUTSIDE PLAY AND LEARNING BOOK

# Glitter Paint Shake

**3+**

*Glitter adds a bit of fun to this activity.*

## Words to use

glitter                 shiny
shake                   cardboard
glue                    shaker
paint                   thick
thin

## Materials

matte board or cardboard
white glue thinned with water, in a cup
paintbrushes
salt or cheese shakers with large holes
powdered tempera paint
glitter

## What to do

1. Paint the entire surface of the matte board or cardboard with thinned white glue.
2. Fill shakers with powdered tempera and glitter.
3. Shake the paint glitter mixture onto the glue.
4. Dry the project for a long time.

## Teaching tips

Powdered tempera can be inhaled. It is a good idea to wear paint filter masks or doctor's masks while shaking this powdered paint. Artists enjoy this. This project takes a long time to dry, so have a shelf or drying area where it can remain undisturbed for several days.

★ Preschool Art

# Shape That Clay 3+

*Children learn to explore ways to shape clay.*

## Words to use

playdough
shape
clay
sculpt
sculptor

## Materials

clay or playdough
storage containers

## What to do

1. Simply supply the clay or the playdough and let the children work with it on their own.
2. Give each child two "oranges" of clay (about two handfuls).
3. Avoid emphasizing finished products. Manipulating the clay or playdough is the object of this activity.

### Teaching tips

Often teachers choose playdough and do not have children work with clay. Potters' clay is available from school and art supply stores. It is messier, but it also has other properties children enjoy. Children enjoy molding the clay, having it dry out a bit, feeling the clay dust on their hands and the sensation of the cool, wet surface of the clay. Natural clay can be fired when children make things for special occasions. (Avoid the modeling clay which has an oil base and is not easily malleable with young fingers.) A large plastic jar is a good storage container. When the children finish with the clay, have them shape it back into large "oranges" and place them into the plastic jar. Then, place a wet paper towel over the clay and put the lid on tightly. Clay washes off the tables easily because it is just dirt and water.

★ STORY S-T-R-E-T-C-H-E-R-S

# Feather Painting                                4+

*This activity encourages children's creativity and improves their small muscle control.*

### Words to use

| | |
|---|---|
| feather | brush |
| paint | picture |

### Materials

feathers
drawing paper
tempera paint

### What to do

1. The children paint a picture using a feather as a brush.
2. Provide a variety of feathers to obtain variation in pictures.

★ WHERE IS THUMBKIN?

# Pressed Flower Cards                            4+

*This project needs to be started a couple of weeks before you want it finished so that the flowers have time to dry. These cards make lovely Mother's Day greetings.*

### Words to use

| | |
|---|---|
| press | dry |
| flatten | glue |
| design | card |
| message | flower |

## Materials

fresh flowers, grasses, weeds, etc.

a flower press or heavy book such as a telephone book

some absorbent paper, such as plain newsprint or
    construction paper

nice paper for the cards—construction paper
    (in pretty spring colors: green, yellow, pink
    or light blue) or watercolor paper

glue sticks, or white glue in small dishes with cot-
    ton swabs

wax paper

crayons

colored pencils

## What to do

1. A couple of weeks before you want to make the cards,
   gather flowers, grasses, weeds and other items to dry. You
   can dry anything; even weeds look lovely. Keep in mind that
   the thicker the item, the less likely it will dry well. For example, a
   dandelion is too fat to dry well, although you can certainly try one as an experiment.
2. Begin pressing the flowers and other items before they wilt, so bring the flower press (or phone
   book) outdoors, or bring the items indoors soon after you've picked them. Arrange them on the
   blotter sheets of the press or between the folded sheets of absorbent paper if you are using a
   heavy book. The pressed flowers dry the way they are placed in the press, so take time to straight-
   en them out and spread the flower petals. The older children love to help with this. Also, place each
   item separately on the paper—do not overlap them. If using a phone book, do not use pages next
   to each other. It is better to leave chunks of pages between each place with flowers.
3. Tighten the fastening screws or belts of the press, or place something heavy on top of the phone
   book—another phone book will do.
4. Carefully check the drying items after several days. When they are ready to use they will actually
   be dry. Then, carefully remove the flowers and store them flat—perhaps between sheets of
   paper—until you are ready to use them. You can add other items to dry. Change the absorbent
   paper when needed.

Note: Drying things from nature is something you can do year round, starting with colorful leaves and
   fall flowers, winter grasses and hardy weeds and springtime buttercups and clover leaves. The tech-
   nique is the same, the children love to do it, and you can build up an accumulation of items to be
   used for cards, tables, decorations, posters or bulletin boards or to put in the Season's Garden.

5. Make cards by folding a sheet of paper in half. Paper 8-1/2 x 11 inches works well, but use any
   size you like. Just don't make it too big or you will use up all the dried flowers very quickly.
6. On the front of the card, the children arrange a few of the dried items, then glue them down. Glue
   sticks are less messy to use, but a dish of white glue with cotton swabs (and reminders to use just a
   little!) will work. Apply the glue lightly to the paper and gently press the flowers onto it.
7. Lay the card between a folded sheet of wax paper so it won't stick, and put it in or under a heavy
   book for 30 minutes or so to give the glue time to dry.
8. The children can draw a picture inside the card. You can write a short message for the children
   using colored pencils, which have a softer, lighter touch.

★ EARTHWAYS

art activities

# Butterfly Pop-up Cards

*This is a simple idea that is very adaptable for any occasion. Simply select other pop-up figures depending on the occasion and interests of the group—birds, rainbows, hearts—and adjust the size of the paper figure to the size of the card. Once the children get the hang of this, be prepared for them to want to fold everything in sight!*

## Words to use

pop
spring
coil
jump out
butterfly
card

cut a few butterfly shapes

Cut strips 3/4" wide by 6-8" long

## Materials

card paper—card stock is very special, but construction paper will do—choose light, springtime colors or have the children use crayons or watercolor paint to color white paper
crayons
construction paper—some cut into little butterflies (see pattern) and some cut into little strips 3/4" wide by 6-8" long
scissors
white glue or glue sticks

## What to do

1. Fold the card paper in half or in quarters to make the size card you want. The size of the butterfly should also vary with the size of the card. The size butterfly illustrated works with an 8-1/2 x 11 inch sheet of paper folded in quarters (in half top to bottom and in half again side to side).
2. Let the children color the front (and maybe the back) cover of the card. If you are using construction paper, be sure to choose lighter colors so the drawing and decorating will show.
3. Give each child a butterfly and a small strip of paper. Show the children how to fold the strip accordion style—front to back, not over and over. This becomes a little paper hinge.
4. Put a small dot of glue on the underside of the butterfly and attach it to the top of the hinge.
5. Glue the bottom of the hinge to the center of the right-hand side of the inside of the card.
6. When you open the card, the butterfly will gently rise up.
7. Make sure the children's names are on their cards. Write a message if desired, or allow the children to decorate the inside of the card with crayons.

Note: You could also have the children do a watercolor painting, then cut out the card and butterfly from the painting. Add lots of water to the colors so you get pale, pastel shades.

★ EARTHWAYS

MAY

art activities

# Tissue Paper Butterflies and Mobiles          **4+**

*These butterflies are simple to make yet very beautiful. Children will love them and may want to make several.*

## Words to use

butterflies
mobile
hang
balance
fly

## Materials

colored tissue paper in light spring colors cut into rectangles 3" x 5", with rounded corners
pipe cleaners—white is nice, but any color will do— approximately 5-6" long
thin string, heavy thread or embroidery floss
scissors
sticks or dowels
pieces of cane
ribbons or crepe paper

## What to do

1. Take two tissue paper rectangles and place one on top of the other. Using two different colors can be nice.
2. Gather them in the center and bind them with a pipe cleaner by twisting it several times around itself. The ends of the pipe cleaner will be the butterfly antennae; the twisted section will be the body.
3. Separate and fluff up the tissue paper wings and bend back the pipe cleaner antennae to shape your butterfly.
4. Tie a heavy thread or light string through the top of the butterfly (go under the top of the pipe cleaner). By holding this string and moving their arms around, the children can make the butterflies fly. Or tie the butterfly's string on the end of a stick. This makes it very special, like a magic wand. Just watch that no one gets poked and that the children aren't running with the sticks—running is for "stickless" butterflies only.
5. A tall vase full of colorful butterflies on sticks or dowels makes a lovely springtime centerpiece.
6. You could also make a lovely butterfly mobile. Bend the caning into a ring (approximately 6-8 inches in diameter) and bind it with heavy thread, string or embroidery floss. Then wrap it with colorful ribbon or crepe paper. Tie the butterflies onto the ring of cane, varying the lengths of string so that they hang at different heights.

7. Using three equal lengths of heavy thread, string or embroidery floss, attach each length to the rim of the ring. Space them equally around the ring so it will be balanced. Gather the ends of the strings together and knot. Have each child make a mobile, and they will enjoy taking them home to share with their families.

★ EARTHWAYS

## Bumble Bee

4+

*Children learn about science and insects, reduce their fear of bees, identify shapes and colors, and improve fine motor skills through a creative experience.*

### Words to use

bee
buzz
antennae
wings
fly
pollinate

### Materials

yellow pompoms
(two per child)
3" pipe cleaners
(one per child)
4" x 4" black
construction
paper
black marker
glue
scissors

### What to do

1. Draw two pairs of wings on the black paper and cut them out (see figure 1).
2. Staple the wings one on top of the other. Glue two yellow pompoms between the wings for the body.
3. Attach the pipe cleaner to make antennae (see figure 2).
4. Draw black horizontal stripes on the pompoms.

★ THE GIANT ENCYCLOPEDIA OF THEME ACTIVITIES

# Claydoh Beads                                    4+

*This activity enhances small motor skills and creativity.*

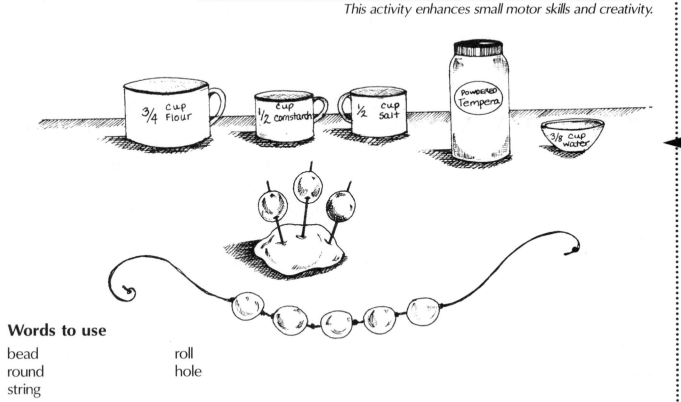

## Words to use

bead                     roll
round                    hole
string

## Materials

3/4 cup flour
1/2 cup cornstarch
1/2 cup salt
powdered tempera or powdered vegetable dye for color
3/8 cup warm water
bowl
toothpicks
string, yarn or leather strips
clear gloss enamel, optional

## What to do

1. Mix flour, cornstarch and salt in a bowl. (Add powdered tempera or powdered vegetable dye for colored dough.) Add warm water slowly until mixture can be kneaded into a stiff dough. Add additional flour to reduce stickiness if necessary.
2. Roll dough into balls for beads.
3. Poke a hole in each ball with a toothpick and dry for a few days. (Large beads take longer to dry.)
4. Paint if desired.
5. If desired, an adult can coat the beads with a clear gloss enamel to make them more durable.
6. When the beads are dry, string them on yarn, string or leather strips. You may tie knots in between each bead.

## Teaching tips

To dry beads, stick toothpicks into a ball of playdough. Place one bead on each toothpick. Twist beads on toothpicks during the drying time to be sure they don't stick to the toothpicks. This recipe makes a fairly smooth dough that keeps its color when dry. A bit of salt residue shows in the beads, especially in darker colored doughs.

★ PRESCHOOL ART

# Shadow Drawing                                    4+

*Shadows are fascinating to watch and fun to draw.*

## Words to use

shadow
dark
light
change
longer
shorter

## Materials

large sheet of butcher paper
felt pens, paints and brushes, crayon or chalk
sunny day outside
4 rocks, optional

## What to do

1. Go for a walk looking for shadows on the ground. Find a shadow that is appealing in design.
2. Place the large sheet of butcher paper on the shadow. Adjust the paper so that the shadow falls on the paper.
3. If the day is windy, place a rock on each corner of the paper to keep it from blowing away.
4. Using any choice of drawing or painting tools, trace, outline, color in or decorate the paper using the shadow as the design.
5. When complete, remove the paper and observe the shadow drawing.

## Want to do more?

Cut the design out and glue it on another sheet of paper of contrasting color. Black is often an effective choice for a background. Make a shadow drawing of a friend's shadow. When using crayon, place textured surfaces behind the paper to add design to the shadow drawing. A wire mesh screen, sheet of plywood, bumpy scrap of vinyl flooring or scrap of Formica make interesting textures.

## Teaching tips

Crayons take a long time on this design activity, but some children enjoy this. Crayons also tend to poke holes in the paper so it helps to have cardboard or a sheet of plywood under the paper as a hard surface. Paint covers fastest. Carry cups of paints and paintbrushes in a flat cardboard box to prevent spilling.

★ PRESCHOOL ART

# Fence Weaving 4+

*Spark children's interest and creativity with this outside art activity using unusual materials.*

## Words to use

weave
in and out
back and forth
decorate
design
fence
strip
ribbon
lace
yarn

## Materials

fence (chain link fences work well)
items for weaving such as crepe paper, strips of fabric, rope, ribbon, lace, strips of newsprint, yarn

## What to do

1. Find a fence that is comfortable to reach and easy to stand beside.
2. Weave and wrap materials through the fence.
3. Continue adding decorations and weaving until the fence is woven and decorated as desired.
4. Remove the weaving before it rains, but enjoy it as long as possible.

## Want to do more?

Make a swing-set or playground equipment weaving. Plan the fence weaving as part of a party, play or special event.

## Teaching tips

One trick to making weaving easier for young artists is to keep the strips fairly short (not more than two or three feet in length). Another more challenging weaving approach is to roll the strips in a ball and place them in a container with a hole at the top. The artist feeds the strips through the fence wire, unrolling it from the container.

★ PRESCHOOL ART

# Circle Time and Group Activities

## Ribbons and Bows

3+

*This activity enhances children's imagination and thinking skills.*

### Words to use

| | |
|---|---|
| guess | hint |
| gift | bows |
| decorate | special |
| box | bag |
| ribbons | color words |
| texture | party |
| celebrate | special occasion |

### Materials

ribbons and bows
large box or bag

### What to do

1. Place the ribbons (cut in various lengths) and the bows in the box or bag and bring it to circle time. Ask the children to guess what is inside.
2. Give the children hints, such as: it is often on top of a birthday gift; it can be tied in a knot; it can be worn in a girl's hair.
3. After the children guess what is in the box or bag, show them the ribbons and bows and talk about how they are used and about the colors and textures.

### Want to do more?

**Art:** Wrap boxes and ask the children to add ribbons and bows for a three-dimensional art project. Invite the children to make collages with the ribbons and bows. Cut a hole in the center of a paper plate and then decorate the plate with ribbons and bows to create a wreath.
**Fine motor:** Encourage the children to tie ribbon in knots.
**Math:** Count and sort the ribbons and bows according to color and texture.
**Social skills:** Plan an Unbirthday Party with the children. Decorate the room with ribbons and bows. Bake an unbirthday cake for snack. Sing "Happy Unbirthday."

★ THE GIANT ENCYCLOPEDIA OF CIRCLE TIME AND GROUP ACTIVITIES

# My Favorite Stuffed Friend

*This activity encourages the development of expressive language skills and social skills.*

## Words to use

favorite
stuffed animal
tell about
story

## Materials

stuffed animals (each child
   brings one from home)
paper, crayons, markers
paint and brushes

## What to do

1. In advance, send a note to parents asking that their child bring a favorite stuffed animal on Favorite Friend Day.
2. At circle time, talk about the children's stuffed animals and ask the children to tell the other children about their animals.

## Want to do more?

**Art:** Ask the children to bring their stuffed animals to the art center. Provide paper and crayons for the children to trace their animals and then color the tracings with crayons, markers or paint.

**Outdoors**: Spread a blanket outdoors and enjoy a picnic with stuffed friends.

★ THE GIANT ENCYCLOPEDIA OF CIRCLE TIME AND GROUP ACTIVITIES

# Slowly, Slowly

3+

*Teaches children about fast and slow.*

## Words to use

| | |
|---|---|
| slowly | quickly |
| creep | up |
| underneath | snail |
| bug | rug |

## What to do

At circle time encourage the children to act out the words of this chant.

MAY

circle time activities

*Slowly, slowly, very slowly,*
*Creeps the garden snail.*
*Slowly, slowly, very slowly,*
*Up the wooden rail. (say the words very, very slowly)*

*Quickly, quickly, very quickly,*
*Creeps the little bug.*
*Quickly, quickly, very quickly,*
*Underneath the rug. (say the words very quickly)*

★ 500 FIVE MINUTE GAMES

# Hot Letters

**5+**

*Children practice letter recognition.*

## Words to use

| | |
|---|---|
| letter | name |
| pass | music |
| stop | direction |
| to the right | to the left |
| around the circle | |

## Materials

index cards with one letter on each

## What to do

1. This is a variation of "Hot Potato."
2. Sit the children in a circle and pass out cards with one letter on each card.
3. Tell the children that you are going to play music.
4. Ask them to pass their cards around the circle while the music is playing.
5. Ask them to stop passing the cards when the music stops.
6. Be sure to practice the direction in which they should pass the cards.
7. When the music stops, ask each child to name the letter on his card.
8. Play this game for number, shape and color recognition also.

★ 500 FIVE MINUTE GAMES

# We Are the Number Train

*Enhances children's numeral recognition.*

## Words to use

one
two
three
four
five
train
cars
march
chant

## Materials

20 rectangles (5" x 9") in a variety of colors
40 small black circles
20 strings

## What to do

1. Before beginning this activity, write the numerals 1 to 5 (four of each numeral) on the rectangles. Glue two black circles on the bottom of each rectangle for the wheels of the train car. (Involve the children in making the train cars.) If possible, laminate the train cars before attaching the strings.
2. At circle time, the teacher distributes one train car to each child and asks him to put the string over his head and wear it like a necklace.
3. The teacher explains that each child will identify the numeral on his train and then join the other children in forming a number train. They will march around the circle chanting: "We are the number train. Watch us say our number names."
4. The teacher walks around the circle saying the chant. At the end of the chant, she stops by a child and asks him to identify his number. If he names the number correctly, the child stands up and holds onto the teacher to form a train. (If the number is incorrectly named, other children tell the child the number name.) The train continues around the circle adding other children until all the children are marching.
5. After all the children are attached to the train, the chant becomes: "We are the number train. We all know our number names."

## Want to do more?

Adapt the activity to make a color train. The children name the color of the train car they are wearing and chant, "We are the color train, watch us say our color names."

★ THE GIANT ENCYCLOPEDIA OF CIRCLE TIME AND GROUP ACTIVITIES

# Dramatic Play Activities

## Fancy Clothes                    3+

*Children learn social skills in this thoroughly enjoyable activity.*

### Words to use

| | |
|---|---|
| dress up | accessories |
| sparkling | outfits |
| May I help you? | Thank you very much. |
| party | celebrate |
| birthday | holiday |
| celebration | necklace |
| tie | |

### Materials

inexpensive shiny metallic fabric
scissors
cardboard
glue
shells, shiny stickers, etc.

### What to do

1. Let the children use clothes from the Housekeeping Center to dress up for a party.
2. Add a few accessories made by the children in the Party Center.
3. Make ties and scarves by cutting pieces from inexpensive shiny metallic or other unusual fabric.
4. Make sparkling necklaces and/or buckles by gluing shells and attaching stickers to a cardboard form.
5. Paint or sprinkle with glitter for additional decoration.
6. The children select outfits and accessories they want to wear to the party.

★ THE COMPLETE LEARNING CENTER BOOK

# Making Party Hats

*Children learn to construct and decorate a party hat.*

## Words to use

party
celebrate
celebration
cone
shape
decorate
Happy Birthday!

## Materials

sheets of construction paper
scissors
scraps of gift-wrap paper and construction paper
stapler
glue sticks
tape
ribbons

## What to do

1. Show the children how to roll a sheet of construction paper into a cone shape.
2. Staple it in place and round off the edge that will be on top of the head.
3. Bring out collage materials, such as scraps of brightly colored construction paper, gift-wrap paper and bits of ribbon.
4. Let the children decorate their party hats by gluing on bits of brightly colored paper and ribbons.
5. Cut ribbons long enough to tie under the children's chins.
6. Staple the ribbons onto the hats and cover the staple with tape so that the paper is reinforced and the ribbon doesn't pull loose from the paper.

★ MORE STORY S-T-R-E-T-C-H-E-R-S

# Pretend Picnic

*Children learn to role play the preparations for a picnic.*

## Words to use

pretend
picnic
prepare
tablecloth
picnic basket

MAY

dramatic play activities

### Materials

*Come to the Meadow* by Anna Grossnickle Hines
picnic basket
plates
plastic glasses
eating utensils
checkered tablecloth and napkins
plastic models of fruits and other food items

### What to do

1. After reading the book to the children, simply supply the props for the role playing.
2. Watch the children role play a *Come to the Meadow* picnic or their own family picnics.
3. Assist children who may have difficulty getting into an on-going play group by pretending to bring in a special guest or a cousin who stopped by.

### Teaching tips

Consider having the picnic basket with you as you read *Come to the Meadow*. If possible, manage some of the other props associated with the story as Mother's gardening hat and gloves, Dad's work gloves, Brother's fishing pole and Sister's mended kite. Rereading the story with the props brings the story alive again.

★ Story S-t-r-e-t-c-h-e-r-s

# Pet Supply Store                                                        3+

*Children learn that caring for animals requires many different supplies.*

### Words to use

pet
store
supplies
sell
pet food

### Materials

*Clifford's Birthday Party* by Norman Bridwell
leashes
bowls
empty dog food and cat food cans
flea collars
chewy toys
traveling cages
blankets
baskets

## What to do

1. After reading the book to the children, turn the housekeeping and dress-up area into a creative dramatics center and call it the "Clifford and Friends Pet Supply Store."
2. Invite parents to send in pet supplies, being careful that they have been thoroughly cleaned.
3. With the children, improvise display areas and materials from around the classroom.
4. Add a cash register, note pads, order blanks, pens and pencils and other supplies for the check-out stand.
5. Leave the pet supply store up for at least a week and the children will add props and invent roles.

## Teaching tips

Add reference materials on different pets and their needs so that the children role play reading to find information and directing their customers to books about pets.

★ MORE STORY S-T-R-E-T-C-H-E-R-S

# A Pet Show                                        4+

*Children learn language skills, organization skills and social skills.*

## Words to use

plan
groom
train
advertise
announcer
judge
ribbon

## Materials

paper
markers
blue construction paper
scissors
"pets" (stuffed animals)

## What to do

1. Help the children plan a pet show.
2. Make fliers advertising the show.
3. The children "groom" and "train" their pets for the big show.
4. An announcer calls the names of the pets; their owners walk around the path.
5. Judges award blue ribbons to all the pets that participate in the show.

★ THE COMPLETE LEARNING CENTER BOOK

# Flower or Leafy Crowns

## 4+

*Sometimes all young children need for a costume is a simple crown, and these crowns make beautiful spring-time costumes. We made extra ones to keep in the classroom, and the children wore them out!*

### Words to use

crown
flowers
leaves

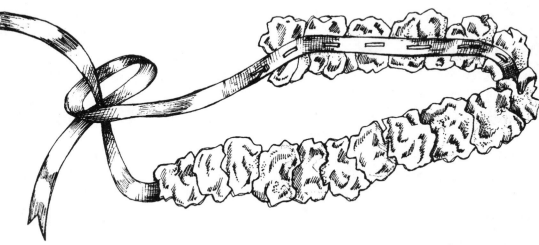

### Materials

ribbons—choose light spring colors: pink, light green, light blue, pale yellow. I used 3/4" wide grosgrain ribbon. It isn't as slippery as the shiny variations and is easier to work with.

tissue paper—again choose light spring colors—although I did use a deeper green and a dark green-blue for Leafy Crowns. Cut the tissue paper into rectangles 2" wide by 5" long and sort according to color.

needles and thread

### What to do

1. Give each child a ribbon cut to fit his or her head (don't forget to add another 8-12 inches for the knot and streamers). Also, give each child a needle knotted and threaded with about 12 inches of doubled thread.

2. Bring the threaded needle up through the ribbon about 7 inches in from the end to allow space for knotting and streamers. This also puts the knot on the back side of the ribbon.

3. Have the children choose a rectangle of colored paper and sew a running stitch lengthwise down the center of it, scrunching it as they go. Then gather this "blossom" or "leaf" by pushing the tissue paper down to the end of the thread. Tack the blossom onto the ribbon by sewing down through the blossom and the ribbon, and then up through the ribbon again so the needle is now on top of the ribbon, ready to stitch another tissue paper blossom.

Note: Help the children fluff and/or scrunch the tissue paper to make it more "blossomy."

4. Continue to gather and stitch these blossoms onto the ribbon until you reach a point seven inches in from the other end of the ribbon. After stitching on the last blossom, knot off the thread on the back of the ribbon. The closer the blossoms, the more beautiful the crown will be. Choose a random selection of colors, or encourage the children to set up a pattern and stick with it—pink, green, yellow; pink, green, yellow or dark blue, dark green; dark blue, dark green. The children enjoy this sequencing, anticipating what will come next.

5. When the ribbon is full of blossoms, except for the knot and the streamer allowance at the end, tie it around the maker's head and marvel at what a beautiful thing they've created!

★ EARTHWAYS

MAY

dramatic play activities

# Miniature Worlds

*When a child creates a miniature world, he must see things in relative sizes. If a block is a house, a pine cone would be big enough to be a tree. This activity is a good imagination builder, and children can work together to solve problems and extend their own ideas.*

## Words to use

world
create
people
building
trees
mountains
tunnel
bridge
lake
river

## Materials

sand shovel
miniature people, animals and/or dinosaurs
small vehicles
pine cones (for miniature pine trees)
pretty stones and rocks
manipulative toys, such as Lincoln logs, tinker toys, craft sticks, plastic drinking straws or wooden blocks
containers to make molds
water, optional

## What to do

1. Simply place these materials (or others) in the sand area.
2. Show the children how to make roads by pushing a wooden block through the sand.
3. Ask the children what they could use to make houses for the people in the town. Let them decide what type of buildings to make and where the roads should go.
4. What could they use for trees or lakes?
5. When sand play seems to become boring, provide a new variety of materials.

## Want to do more?

Let the children create a scene and tell a story as they move things around in their little town. Or let them create a setting for a familiar story, such as "Goldilocks and the Three Bears" and then enact the story that they have created.

★ THE OUTSIDE PLAY AND LEARNING BOOK

MAY

dramatic play activities

# Language Activities

## Rhyming Words Match

4+

*Encourages children's auditory discrimination and numeral recognition.*

### Words to use

rhyme
sounds the same
numbers
song

### Materials

pictures of items that rhyme
index cards with the numbers 1-10 written on them

### What to do

1. Talk about the rhyming words in the song, "The Ants Go Marching" (words on page 170).
2. Ask the children to match pictures of items that rhyme.
3. If pictures can be found of items mentioned in the song, for example, a shoe, gate or door, have children match pictures to the correct numeral card.

★ WHERE IS THUMBKIN?

## On Stage

4+

*This activity introduces the alphabet to children.*

### Words to use

alphabet
letter names
card
necklace

### Materials

squares of cardboard, approximately 8" x 8"
markers
lengths of string

## What to do

1. Draw large letters on each of 26 squares of cardboard. Attach each letter to a string to make a necklace. Give one card necklace to each child. (If the class is small, teacher can substitute by taking excess letters.)
2. Teacher announces each alphabet letter with "Ladies and Gentlemen, may I present 'Mister A,'" etc.
3. As each letter is announced, the child goes to the front of the room and performs an activity of his choice, such as jumping up and down, twirling around, bowing, etc.

★ THE INSTANT CURRICULUM

# Slinky Letters 4+

*Children practice letter recognition skills.*

## Words to use

letter names
feel
tactile
starch

## Materials

line drawings of letters
yarn cut into short lengths
bowl of liquid starch

## What to do

1. Provide a large line drawing of an alphabet letter for each child.
2. Children dip a length of yarn into a bowl of liquid starch.
3. The yarn is placed on the letter configuration.
4. When dry, a tactile letter has been formed.

★ THE INSTANT CURRICULUM

# Sand Letters 4+

*This activity practices letter recognition skills.*

## Words to use

alphabet          letter names
sand              rough
feel              texture

## Materials

index cards with a letter drawn on each
glue
cotton swabs or Q-tips
sand

## What to do

1. Provide children with cards that have a large alphabet letter drawn on them.
2. Give children a Q-tip to apply glue to the outline of the letter.
3. Have children sprinkle sand over the glue and shake off excess. A three-dimensional letter is created to use and reuse for letter recognition.

★ THE INSTANT CURRICULUM

# Lacing Letter                    4+

*Children practice small motor skills while learning the letters.*

## Words to use

alphabet
letter names
holes
punch
sew
in and out
cardboard
outline
cut out
shape
lace

## Materials

cardboard pieces
scissors
hole punch
yarn cut into 2' lengths

## What to do

1. Draw one letter on each piece of cardboard. Cut out along the outline.
2. Punch holes in the outline of each letter about one inch apart.
3. Attach a two foot piece of yarn to the letter.
4. Allow children to lace the outline of the letter.

★ THE INSTANT CURRICULUM

# Our Class Alphabet

*Children practice letter recognition.*

## Words to use

photograph
picture
letter
first
starts with
book

## Materials

photograph of
  each child
construction
  paper (various
  colors)
magazines or toy
  catalogs

## What to do

1. Cut construction paper in half. Use one half page for each child.
2. On each page glue the photograph of an individual child. Under the picture print the first letter of the child's name. Under that letter print the child's first name. Repeat for each child in the class.
3. Arrange the pages in alphabetical order. It is all right to have a number of children with the same first letter in their names.
4. Determine which letters are missing, for example, you probably won't have any children whose names start with Q, X or Z.
5. Use magazines or toy catalogs to find colored pictures of objects that start with the missing letters and make a page for each letter, so that each letter of the alphabet has at least one page with either a photograph of a child or a picture of an object that starts with that letter.
6. Read aloud the "Class Alphabet Book." Encourage the children to "read" the book aloud: "A for Allison, B for Bill," etc. Make the book available for them to look at during playtime.

## Want to do more?

**Language:** Let the children take turns taking the "Class Alphabet Book" home to read with their families. When a new child or parent volunteer joins the class, ask that person to take the book home. It is a great way to learn the names of the children in the class. Have double prints made of the photographs and use the second set in the same way for a bulletin board.

## Books to read

*Anno's Alphabet* by Anno Mitsmasa
*Dr. Seuss ABC's* by Dr. Seuss
*On Market Street* by Arnold Lobel

MAY

language activities

# 1, 2, 3, Hush

**4+**

*There is a world full of sounds that shouldn't be missed, like the slight trickle of a rivulet, the gentle chirp of a song sparrow or the wind in the trees. The purpose of this activity is to emphasize the value of listening to gentle sounds as a means of getting to know our world.*

## Words to use

| | |
|---|---|
| auditory | quiet |
| sounds | look |
| listen | gentle |
| nature | natural |
| bird | chirp |
| sing | explore |

## Materials

proper dress
sit-upon
tape recorder

## What to do

1. This activity requires a walk to a site that is fairly isolated from human activities.
2. The walk should be a normal exploration activity with the children involved in visual exploration.
3. As you approach the isolated site, the group should be stopped and asked not to talk and to walk quietly.
4. Using this orderly quiet walk, move to the isolated location and find a spot where the group can sit and listen. The key here is a comfortable position for each participant: lying flat on the ground or sitting or leaning against a tree are usually best. On the count of 3 everyone stops talking and stays very still. For two to three minutes listen to the sounds of the place. When the quiet time is finished, discuss what was heard and the children's feelings about the experience.

## Want to do more?

Compare the sounds to music. What could be used to create similar sounds? What sounds did each person like? Compare natural to man-made sounds. How did each make you feel? Try the listening activity in different areas. Make lists of the sounds in different places and compare them. Record various sounds. How do you feel when man-made sounds invade the quiet natural environment? Make one minute tapes in various settings. Can you identify them later? Do sounds matter to wild animals? How? Imagine that you are a rabbit. What could a sound tell you? What sounds are important to a hunting animal (fox)—to a hunted animal (rabbit)?

★ Hug a Tree

# Know Talk

*Be prepared to experience some frustration when trying to communicate with children without words. As with other sensory deprivation activities, working through their frustrations is an important part of the experience.*

## Words to use

help
talk
communicate
sign language
describe
motion

## Materials

## What to do

1. Ask the children to tell you why being able to talk is important. How would they feel if they could never talk with words? Mention that some people cannot talk because the parts of their bodies that make a voice do not work correctly.
2. Introduce the idea of sign language: talking with hands and other parts of the body. Demonstrate several examples and ask the children to identify what you are trying to tell them—
   ✓ Shake head yes
   ✓ Shake head no
   ✓ Shake a tight fist and make an angry face
   ✓ Wave good-bye
   ✓ Extend both arms as an invitation to hug.
3. Tell the children that you want to find out what it would be like to be a person who cannot talk in their classroom. When you finish describing this activity, you will pretend for the rest of the morning that you cannot talk. If you have something to tell them, you will say it with your hands and facial expressions.
4. For the rest of the morning, if speaking is necessary, motion to another teacher or aide to talk for you. At the end of your experiment, discuss with the children what happened.

## Want to do more?

Invite the children to explore how they make sounds. Ask them to touch their throats while making different sounds, talk while pinching their noses shut or talk with their tongues sticking out. Emphasize that many different parts of the body contribute to making speech sounds. Invite a sign language expert to visit your class and teach the children a few basics of that language.

## Home connection

Parents can play a similar game of sign language with their children. With older children, they can try signing an entire conversation over dinner.

★ THE PEACEFUL CLASSROOM

MAY

language activities

# Old Lady Puppet

**5+**

*This activity teaches children sequencing skills.*

## Words to use

puppet
swallow
fly
spider
bird
cat
dog
cow
horse

## Materials

scissors
6" x 12" paper bags
plastic acetate or vinyl
tape
poster board
stapler
paper plate
crayons
cotton balls
construction paper
index cards

cut a 6X6" square on front or back of a paper bag.

7"  7"

tape a 7X7" piece of acetate inside the bag to cover the 6" square opening.

decorate a paper plate as face. add cotton balls for hair and staple to bottom of bag.

add arms and hands and staple to bag.

cut a slit on side of bag large enough for a hand.

cut index cards in two and draw things the "old lady" ate in the song.

place a second grocery bag the opposite way inside the first and staple together at the bottom.

add legs and feet and staple to bag.

## What to do

1. To make a see-through old lady with the children, cut a 6 x 6 inch square out of the front or back of the paper bag. Tape a 7 x 7 inch piece of acetate inside the bag to cover the 6-inch square opening.
2. Decorate a paper plate as a face. Add cotton balls for hair and staple on the bottom flap of the bag (the head of the "old lady").
3. Cut legs and arms from poster board and staple on the bag in the correct places.
4. Cut hands and shoes from construction paper and attach with a stapler or tape.
5. Place a second grocery sack the opposite way inside the first sack and staple together at the bottom.
6. Cut a slit through the sides of the two bags, large enough to fit a hand.
7. Cut index cards in two and draw things the old lady ate in the song "There Was an Old Lady" on them.
8. Sing the song, feeding the old lady as you sing.
9. Retrieve cards from the side slit after you have finished.

★ WHERE IS THUMBKIN?

# Math Activities

## Scavenger Hunt

3+

*This activity enhances children's observation skills and problem solving skills.*

### Words to use

scavenger          find
search             mark
work together      partner

### Materials

paper with pictures of hidden items
copies for each child
markers

### What to do

1. On one sheet of paper the teacher draws pictures of items that have been hidden in the Party Center.
2. Each child has a copy of this sheet and a marker.
3. When a child finds an item, he places a mark next to the picture of the item on his sheet.
4. The children work individually or with a partner on the scavenger hunt.
5. Some children may wish to repeat the scavenger hunt. This time they can make their own sheets for finding items that they have hidden in the center.

★ THE COMPLETE LEARNING CENTER BOOK

## Duck Pond

3+

*Encourages children's visual memory and color recognition skills.*

### Words to use

duck       pond
swim       color words
pairs      two that match

## Materials

eight rubber or plastic ducks
tub
water
colored tape (red, blue, green, yellow)

## What to do

1. Place a piece of colored tape on the bottom of each duck. Create pairs by using two pieces of each color tape.
2. Float the ducks in the tub.
3. The children name a color and then pick up two ducks in an attempt to find matching colors.

★ WHERE IS THUMBKIN?

# It's an Animal                    3+

*Children sort a variety of objects or pictures into categories: animals or not animals.*

## Words to use

sort
It's an animal.
It isn't an animal.

## Materials

plastic replicas or photographs of animals
other objects or pictures of objects

## What to do

1. Put the objects or pictures into a container or basket or spread them on a work surface.
2. Present the objects or pictures to the children.
3. Have the children sort the objects or pictures according to whether or not "It's an animal!"

## Want to do more?

Focus the children's attention on specific features of the objects or pictures in order to verbalize specific characteristics of animals. Encourage the children to think of their own examples of "animal" or "not animal." For a more advanced activity, sort them into groups according to different kinds of animals.

★ THE GIANT ENCYCLOPEDIA OF THEME ACTIVITIES

# Would You Let a Caterpillar Crawl on Your Hand?

**3+**

*Children learn to make a simple graph and to compare the numbers of yes's and no's.*

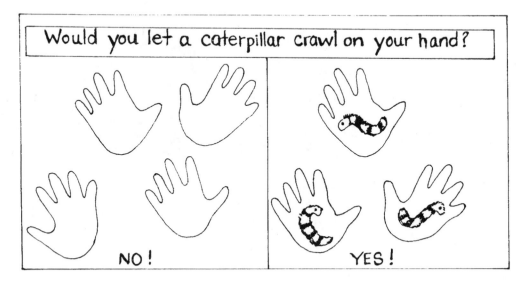

## Words to use

| caterpillar | crawl |
| cut out | chart |
| graph | yes |
| no | |

## Materials

*The Very Hungry Caterpillar* by Eric Carle
construction paper     poster board
glue or tape     pencils or crayons
scissors

## What to do

1. Read the book, then ask who would let a caterpillar crawl on their hand. Ask these children to draw around each other's hands, cut out the hand shapes and then draw a caterpillar on their hands. For the children who answered no, leave the hands blank.
2. Construct a chart with a yes and no column.
3. Have the children place the hands with the caterpillar in the "yes" column and the hands without the caterpillar in the "no" column.
4. Compare the simple graph and determine which column has more responses.

## Teaching tips

Young preschoolers will count a few hands and simply say this one has "more" than the other chart. The older children will be able to count and actually make the numerical comparison.

★ STORY S-T-R-E-T-C-H-E-R-S

# Buzz, Buzz

*This activity develops premath skills.*

### Words to use

bees
buzz
beehive
home

### Materials

white poster board
scissors
contact paper or laminating
   film, optional
colored markers
pencils
glue

① enlarge and make
3 copies of beehive.

② enlarge and
make copies
of bees.

### What to do

1. Copy the illustrations, color them and glue them to the poster board or oaktag. Cut them out and, if you really want them to last, laminate them.
2. Place the three hives on the table in front of the children. Hold up two bees and say, "These bees went buzzing over to this hive, looking for a nice place to live." Lay the bees on one hive.
3. Hold up one bee and say, "This bee decided to go buzzing over to this hive." Lay the bee on another hive.
4. Hold up three bees and say, "These three bees thought that this hive looked like a nice home." Lay the bees on the remaining hive.
5. Indicate the three hives. Ask which of the hives has the most bees on it. If the children have a difficult time answering, count the bees on each hive and ask again.

### Want to do more?

You can extend this activity by playing a version of the game "Pin the Tail on the Donkey." Make extra copies of the bees and have the children color and cut them out. At the same time, draw a large version of the hives on three pieces of poster board, color them and cut them out. Mount the hives on a wall right next to each other at the children's eye level, put a piece of rolled up masking tape on the back of each bee, and you're ready to play. Play should proceed as a normal game of "Pin the Tail on the Donkey" would. Blindfold each child in turn and have them pin their bee on any of the three hives (whichever one they can "find" in the dark). After each child has had a turn, have them count the number of bees that landed on each hive. Then ask again, "Which hive has the most bees on it?" To simplify this activity for younger toddlers, reduce the number of hives used to two. You also might want to eliminate use of the blindfold, since young children do not often enjoy not being able to see.

## Books to read

*Count and See* by Tana Hoban
*One Two Three: An Animal Counting Book* by Marc Brown
*I Is One* by Tasha Tudor

★ THE GIANT ENCYCLOPEDIA OF THEME ACTIVITIES

# Variations of Five                                    4+

*This activity begins to teach children about numeration—with an understanding of five.*

## Words to use

combination
one
two
three
four
five
move
beans

## Materials

lima beans
sealable sandwich bag
marker

## What to do

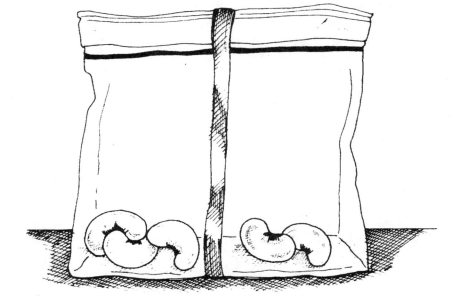

1. Place five lima beans in a sealable sandwich bag.
2. Draw a vertical line down the middle of the bag (extending from the top to the bottom of the bag).
3. Encourage the children to manipulate the beans on either side of the line to see all the combinations of five.

★ WHERE IS THUMBKIN?

# Sequencing

**4+**

*This activity teaches children about sequencing and size relationship.*

**Words to use**

size
largest
smallest
sequence

**Materials**

pictures of each item
the old lady (in the
song "There Was An
Old Lady") swal-
lowed or small plastic
animals/insects rep-
resenting each animal
swallowed

**What to do**

1. Ask children to sequence the animals or animal pictures from smallest to largest.
2. Ask them if this is the order in which the old lady swallowed the animals.

★ Where Is Thumbkin?

# Five Lost

**4+**

*Children learn to count five objects in a set and to recognize when something is missing.*

**Words to use**

set
missing
find
Where can it be?

**Materials**

*Where Can It Be?* by Ann Jonas
several groups of five things that are easily found in the classroom, such as five puzzle pieces, five
    crayons from a box, five missing snacks, five hiding children

**What to do**

1. Play "Where can it be?" with sets of five things. Throughout the day, hide five things. For example,
    when you place a puzzle out on the table, have five pieces missing. At the art table, have five
    crayons missing from the box. At circle time, hide five children behind a room divider. At outdoor
    play time, hide five coats. At snack time, leave five snacks off the table.

2. Then have different children search for the missing objects by going round and asking, "Where can they be?" just like the little girl in the book.
3. Give hints to the child by using the old ploy of "You're getting hot" when the child is close and "You're getting cold" when the child is far away from the hidden objects.
4. After the child finds the missing five, have her count them and return the objects to their proper places.

## Teaching tips

For a young preschooler, hide the items or children in obvious places and direct the child to the area where she is to look. For older preschoolers, let them take turns hiding five objects and playing the game throughout the day. Remember to keep the element of surprise going by suddenly having five things missing throughout the day.

★ STORY S-T-R-E-T-C-H-E-R-S

# Who's Got More?                    4+

*As children play in this way, they gradually learn about different volumes and shapes and become more accurate in their guesses. Children may also learn concepts such as more, less, too much, not enough, full, heavy, big and little, as they play.*

## Words to use

| | |
|---|---|
| container | size |
| volume | holds more |
| holds less | full |
| empty | heavy |
| light | big |
| little | quart |
| pint | |

## Materials

dry sand
several containers of obviously different volumes, such as a measuring cup, a quart pitcher and a pint pitcher
spoon or shovel

## What to do

1. Ask the children if they think the containers are the same size and will hold the same amount of sand. If not, which is biggest or will hold the most sand? Which holds the next most sand? Which holds the least sand?
2. Then ask the children how to test their guesses.
3. Let the children come up with their own test measure. They might suggest seeing how many small containers it takes to fill each larger container. They could suggest filling one container and pouring the contents into another container. How will we know if the first container has more sand? Do this with a lot of different containers so the children learn about overflowing containers and making comparisons.

## Want to do more?

After a while, ask the children if they can think of other ways to make the test. Try using a balance scale. Do this exercise using many different types, shapes and weights of containers. Let several children do this on their own, forming their own conclusions, rather than only with an adult. With older children who have a concept of number, you might ask the children to guess how many of a smaller container will fill a larger container, and then test their guesses. Vary the experience by providing different containers from time to time.

★ THE OUTSIDE PLAY AND LEARNING BOOK

# What Shape Comes Next? 4+

*This activity helps children learn about sequencing, to think about what comes first, next and last. To repeat the pattern, the child must compare, think about same and different and think about the whole pattern set. This type of activity helps form the abstract thinking base necessary for mathematics.*

## Words to use

shape
mold
pattern
What comes next?

## Materials

two or three different containers to make sand mold shapes, such as a stocking egg half, a tomato sauce can and a plastic rectangle soap holder

## What to do

1. With the children watching, start making a pattern with the molds. Example: egg, egg, can; egg, egg, can; egg.... Then stop and ask the children which container you should use next.
2. See if the children can tell you the correct containers to use to continue the sequence.
3. Then let a child become the maker, continuing the sequence to make a long pattern.

## Want to do more?

Use different containers each day to make different patterns. When the activity becomes easy, make more complex patterns using more shapes: A, A, B, C; A, A, B, C or A, B, A, B, C, D, D; A, B, A, B, C, D, D. See if the child can reproduce the same pattern (A, B, B; A, B, B) using different materials, such as sticks and stones or leaves and acorns. Let the children make "fences" and long "snakes" of patterns. Encourage them to make up their own patterns and to think of different materials to use.

★ THE OUTSIDE PLAY AND LEARNING BOOK

# Treasure Hunt for Golden Pebbles

*Children practice counting with this activity. Additionally, you can introduce them to balance scales and the concept of weighing.*

## Words to use

treasure
golden
bury
hunt
find
dig
hide
stone
pebble

## Materials

a quantity of small stones
gold spray paint
sand

## What to do

1. If the children are old enough, let them help you spray paint the stones gold.
Note: Do this outside, and be sure to stand upwind of the paint! The paint dries quickly so the teacher should manipulate the paint can.
2. When one side is dry let the children turn the stones over. Spray the other side, keeping in mind the cautions mentioned in step one.
3. When the children are not around, bury the stones in the sand area.
4. The children go on a "treasure hunt" and see how many gold stones they can find.

## Want to do more?

Give the children sifters to help them find the buried stones. Have them count their stones to see who found the most. Or have the children weigh their stones with a balance scale to see who has the heaviest collection of found stones.

★ THE OUTSIDE PLAY AND LEARNING BOOK

# On the Trail of Fives

*We all know that rote memorization of number concepts does not ensure understanding. Children learn best by doing and redoing activities that reinforce the concept of numbers. This activity presents a delightful approach to teaching number concepts. We've used five for our example. Choose a number for your group that is right for them.*

## Words to use

count
find
number
trail
follow
group
path
stop
walk
station
objects
fingers
toes
remember

## Materials

objects from out of doors, grouped in fives
cardboard hands to be used as pointers

## What to do

1. Make a trail for the children to explore. A straight sidewalk or circular path would be easy to use.
2. Prepare stations along the trail. Here are some possibilities: piles of leaves, sticks, rocks, feathers, pine cones, seed pods, sweet gum balls, grass, weeds, dandelions.
3. Prepare the 5's walk by placing a pointing finger above each station.
4. Talk with the children about the number 5. Count the number of fingers and toes. Count to 5.
5. Take the children to the 5's trail. Show them the finger pointer and how it points to a trail.
6. Go from pointer to pointer. Count out five objects at each pointer. What are they called? Why are they all alike? What makes them alike?
7. Go through all the stations.
8. Return to the classroom. See if the children can remember all the stations. What did they find at all the stations? The teacher should list the stations on a large piece of paper as they are remembered.

## Want to do more?

Use different numbers and new stations. Create a 1-10 trail.

★ MORE MUDPIES TO MAGNETS

# Music and Movement Activities

## Party Piñata

*Children learn how to play with a piñata as part of a birthday celebration.*

### Words to use

piñata
break open
treats

### Materials

*Clifford's Birthday Party* by Norman Bridwell
piñata
scarf
yardstick
blindfold

### What to do

1. Show the children the part of *Clifford's Birthday Party* where he is blindfolded and hits the piñata until it breaks.
2. Uncover the piñata from where you have it hidden under a scarf.
3. Hang the piñata in a place where it is safe for one child at a time to hit it.
4. Let the children take turns hitting the piñata with the yardstick until it bursts, spreading its contents on the floor.
5. Then the children can enjoy scrambling for the treats, candies or little toys that were inside. Ask the children to take only one treat.

### Teaching tips

This activity is a good one to do outside by tying the piñata from a tree limb. For young children, do not use a blindfold. Older children can make a piñata as an art project.

★ MORE STORY S-T-R-E-T-C-H-E-R-S

MAY

music & movement activities

# Animal Antics                                        3+

*Children learn to make movements and sounds to accompany scenes from* Baby Animals.

## Words to use

baby animals
read
book
birds
chirp
flutter
flap

## Materials

*Baby Animals* by Margaret Wise Brown

## What to do

1. Highlight some of the animal and bird movements from the book by rereading several pages.
2. Ask the children to make the movements and sounds they think of when they hear the words. For instance, they can flutter and flap their wings, open their beaks and make a chirp like the birds waking up. Or they might roll on their backs like the little pigs and oink and squeal for their breakfast.
3. After they have practiced their movements, reread the book and pause after each scene for the children to act out the motions and sounds.

## Teaching tips

Younger children will want to act out each scene with animal movements and sounds. Older children can volunteer for different scenes. Several children can do each scene so that everyone in the class participates.

★ MORE STORY S-T-R-E-T-C-H-E-R-S

# Monkey See, Monkey Do                                3+

*Develops children's visual memory.*

## Words to use

monkey          leader
copy            follow
action          imitate

## Materials

## What to do

1. Appoint one child to be the lead monkey.
2. The leader performs a series of actions to be copied by the group.
3. Then the leader picks a new leader, and the activity can be repeated.

★ WHERE IS THUMBKIN?

# Butterfly Wings

**3+**

*Children learn how butterflies move.*

## Words to use

butterfly
fly
flutter
wings
streamers
cuff
dance
move

## Materials

10"-15" streamers
computer paper or other
    paper
tape
recorded music

## What to do

1. Tape four or five 10" to
    15" streamers on a piece of
    computer paper.
2. Form into two long cuffs for each child's lower arm and tape, being sure that the streamers are
    flowing freely.
3. When music is played, children can move around the room, fluttering their "wings."

★ THE INSTANT CURRICULUM

# Creepy Caterpillars

*Children learn about caterpillars and how they move.*

## Words to use

caterpillar          crawl
creep               slow

## Materials

## What to do

1. Talk about caterpillars and look at several pictures of them.
2. Have children lie on the floor and move the way caterpillars move, creeping and crawling.
3. Children can pretend to make a cocoon and then come out of the cocoon and pretend to fly away as butterflies to demonstrate the life cycle of a butterfly.

★ THE INSTANT CURRICULUM

# Fireflies

**3+**

*Children learn to move in response to the music.*

## Words to use

fireflies            meadow
on and off          flash

## Materials

flashlights
slow swaying music
record or tape player

## What to do

1. Tell the children that fireflies also live in the meadow.
2. Discuss how fireflies shine their lights.
3. Darken the room and slowly turn a flashlight on and off.
4. Begin the music and gently move the flashlight across the ceiling of the classroom, occasionally turning it off and then back on like the firefly.
5. Have the children sway gently back and forth either seated or standing while the music is playing.
6. After they seem to have the rhythm of the music, give flashlights to three or four children and let them move their lights in response to the music.
7. Stop the music and give the flashlights to other children, or keep the music playing and gently take the light from one child and pass it to another.

## Teaching tips

Place colored tissue paper over the flashlights to create the effect of a misty summer night.

★ STORY S-T-R-E-T-C-H-E-R-S

*MAY*

*music & movement activities*

# From Egg to Caterpillar to Pupa to Butterfly    3+

*Children learn to think of motions which express how each stage of the butterfly's life feels.*

## Words to use

| | |
|---|---|
| egg | creeper |
| balance | shed |
| skin | rest |
| fly | butterfly |
| change | dart |
| soar | move |
| still | whisper |
| quiet | feet |

## Materials

*Where Butterflies Grow* by Joanne Ryder

## What to do

1. Set the tone of the creative drama by having the children curl up and make themselves as tiny as they can be. Darken the room slightly and begin to read the book in almost a whisper.
2. Switch the lights on when the creeper bursts from the egg into the sunlight.
3. Have the children imagine how it feels as a creeper, balancing on tiny leaves with two rows of feet.
4. Ask the children to take a deep breath, puff out their cheeks, arch their backs and pretend to shed a layer of skin.
5. In a whisper, tell the children to stay very still, not moving a muscle while avoiding the beak of a hungry bird.
6. Then have them dramatically take a deep breath and blow it out, pretending to spray a strong smell so the bird goes away.
7. Let the children rest quietly, curled up slightly, then stretch one arm out and pretend to form a "silken sling" to attach themselves to a branch.
8. Have them rest in this position for what seems like a long time, then gradually start to move.
9. Ask them to begin gently moving their arms until they are ready to fly, slowly at first, then soar and fly around, landing at will.
10. Have them land on a flower, perch on all fours, put their heads down and pretend to drink sweet nectar before darting off to another flower and then to soar again.

## Teaching tips

Plan this creative dramatic experience more than once during the week so that children have a chance to improvise more movements.

★ MORE STORY S-T-R-E-T-C-H-E-R-S

music & movement activities

# Five Little Ducks

*Sing or act out Five Little Ducks in just a few minutes. Children enjoy performing, and they will learn number concepts as they sing.*

## Words to use

duck
waddle

## Materials

## What to do

1. Practice singing this song, then select five children to be the baby ducks, one to be momma duck and one to be daddy duck.

> *Five little ducks (hold up five fingers)*
> *Went out to play (flap arms like wings)*
> *Over the hills (move arm up and down)*
> *And far away. (hand over eyes)*
> *The momma duck (make beak with hands)*
> *Called, "Quack, quack, quack,"*
> *And four little ducks (hold up four fingers)*
> *Came waddling back. (flap arms like wings)*
> *Four little ducks....*

2. Continue singing until there are no little ducks left.

> *No little ducks*
> *Went out to play*
> *Over the hills*
> *And far away.*
> *The daddy duck (use both arms to make a big beak)*
> *Called, "QUACK-QUACK-QUACK-QUACK," (say with a loud voice)*
> *And five little ducks*
> *Came waddling back.*

## Want to do more?

Make duck headbands or paper wings for the children to wear as they dramatize the song.

★ TRANSITION TIME

# Jump Ropes

## 3+

*There are many things that children can do with a jump rope besides the traditional jump rope games, which are often too difficult for younger children.*

## Words to use

| | |
|---|---|
| rope | jump |
| tightrope walker | backward |
| forward | curve |
| eyes shut | feel |
| sideways | hop |
| flip | |

## Materials

jump rope

## What to do

Be sure that ropes are well supervised on the playground, and don't allow the children to play games of tying up people. The following are suggestions.

**Tightrope Walk**. Lay the rope in a straight line on the ground. Invite the children to walk along the rope, pretending they are tightrope walkers.

**Backwards Walk**. See if the children can walk backwards on the rope, not stepping off of it.

**Curving Line**. Place the rope in a curving line, and let the children walk forward and backwards along it.

**Eyes Shut**. Challenge the children to walk slowly along the rope with their eyes shut. They must feel the rope with their feet.

**Jump**. Have the children jump across the rope with both feet together. Then see if they can jump backwards across the rope with both feet together.

**Jump Sideways**. Jump across the rope sideways with both feet at once. Then jump back again. Then see if they can do a continuous side to side jumping over the rope, not pausing in between jumps.

**Double Jump**. Jump two times on each side of the rope, and then jump over it. Repeat.

**Hop**. Hop on one foot over the rope and back again. Then use the other foot.

**Flip and Jump**. Have one child hold the ends of the rope, one in each hand, with the middle of the rope on the ground behind him. Then have the child flip the rope forward over his head to land on the ground in front of him and jump over it. Repeat, while moving forward. Do the above, but jump over the rope with one foot, alternating with each jump.

★ THE OUTSIDE PLAY AND LEARNING BOOK

MAY

music & movement activities

# Do Things Four Times

**4+**

*This activity helps children internalize the meaning of the number four.*

## Words to use

four
times
move
repeat
movement
count
clap
sit

## Materials

## What to do

1. Explain that the children will repeat a movement four times.
2. Begin by asking the children to hop four times.
3. Then ask the children what they would like to do next.
4. Continue the activity until all the children have a turn naming the movement. Count to four as you repeat each movement, such as clapping, touching your nose, sitting down.

## Want to do more?

During each day of the week, increase the number of times the children do a movement, such as on Monday do it one time, on Tuesday, two times, etc.
**Language:** Find the numeral four on the wall, in a book, etc.
**Math:** Count a variety of objects into groups of four.
**Outdoors:** Play a game outdoors hunting for four things of the same kind.

## Books to read

*One, Two, One Pair* by Bruce McMillan
*Ten Black Dots* by Donald Crews

## Song to sing

"Four Little Monkeys"

★ THE GIANT ENCYCLOPEDIA OF CIRCLE TIME AND GROUP ACTIVITIES

# Back Stand

*A competitive environment increases tension and frustration and can trigger aggressive behavior among the winners as well as the losers. This activity emphasizes cooperation, not competition.*

## Words to use

cooperate
partner
interlocked
together
effort
back
lift
push
work
pull
stand

## Materials

## What to do

1. Ask the children to form partnerships. Tell them that you would like to see how well they can cooperate. Ask partners to sit back-to-back. When they are ready, ask them to stretch out and interlock their arms with their partner's. You will probably have to demonstrate this.
2. When their arms are interlocked, ask them to work together to stand without letting go of their partner's arms.
3. When the children are finished, ask them to sit facing each other with their legs slightly bent and their feet touching. They should then take hold of each other's hands. Can they pull each other up to a standing position?
4. Encourage the children in their efforts. Comment encouragingly on their attempts to cooperate.

## Want to do more?

Try having three or four children sit back-to-back and stand with their arms interlocked. Then ask these larger groups to sit facing each other, take the hands of two others in the group, and lift each other to a standing position.

## Home connection

Parents and children can try passing an egg to each other from one teaspoon to another.

★ THE PEACEFUL CLASSROOM

MAY

music & movement activities

# Lucky Letters

**4+**

*This activity teaches children letter recognition.*

### Words to use

alphabet
letter names
circle
around
stop
order
walk

### Materials

one set of 26 large index cards with one letter written on each
one set of 26 small index cards with one letter written on each
recorded music

### What to do

1. Write alphabet letters on each of 26 large cards. Make a matching set of small cards.
2. Place large cards on the floor in a circle in alphabetical order.*
3. Put on a record and have the children walk around the circle of cards.
4. When the music stops, each child picks up the letter card closest to her.
5. Teacher holds up the small card with an alphabet letter. Example: H—Child holding H comes into the middle of the circle and sits.

★ THE INSTANT CURRICULUM

# Science Activities

## Pouring Experiments                                      3+

*Children learn control of hand muscles when they learn to pour. They may also discover a little bit about gravity, that pouring sand falls down and will not go up in tubes. When pouring, children are also experimenting with the concepts of empty, full, large, small, narrow, wide, in and out.*

### Words to use

| | |
|---|---|
| empty | full |
| large | narrow |
| wide | in |
| out | up |
| down | pour |
| sand | water |
| pitcher | funnel |

### Materials

various sizes of plastic bottles, with small and large openings
other containers to pour sand into
small plastic pitchers
funnels

### What to do

1. Let the children fill the pitchers with sand and then try to pour it into the bottles without the funnels. What happens?
2. Show the children how to use the funnels, and just let them experiment on their own for a while.
3. The children will discover that they don't need the funnel to pour the sand back into the pitcher from the bottle.

### Want to do more?

Use a permanent marking pen or piece of tape to make lines at various levels on the bottles. Challenge a child to pour sand just up to the line. Add plastic tubing and pipe to the materials and see how the children use them.

★ The Outside Play and Learning Book

# Whose Baby Am I?

*Children learn to associate baby animals with their parents.*

## Words to use

baby
parent
match
pictures
column

## Materials

pictures of baby animals
   and their parents
poster board
magnetic tape
glue
clear contact paper or
   laminating film, optional

## What to do

1. Let the children cut out pictures of baby animals and their parents from old magazines, calendars or coloring books.
2. Cover the pictures with clear contact paper or laminating film.
3. Attach a piece of magnetic tape to each animal picture.
4. Make a poster with two columns, one marked babies and the second marked parents.
5. Place a strip of magnetic tape down each column.
6. Let the children match the baby animals to their parents.

## Teaching tips

Have more babies than adults. Mix the types of pictures so that there may be two colts, one from a calendar picture and one from a coloring book, but include only one parent. Also use different breeds of cats, dogs and other animals to make the task more challenging.

★ MORE STORY S-T-R-E-T-C-H-E-R-S

*MAY*

*science activities*

# Hives and Honeycombs

*Children learn that bees make honey and store it in the honeycomb inside the hive.*

## Words to use

bees
hives
honeycomb
honey
sweet
taste
sticky
clear
magnify
design
beekeeper

## Materials

jar of honey with comb inside
magnifying glasses
an old beehive from the woods
a man-made hive, optional
children's reference book on bees
honeycomb
small linking blocks, if available

## What to do

1. Discuss how bees collect pollen from flowers and turn it into honey.
2. Encourage the children to examine the honeycomb closely with their magnifying glasses and to notice the way each little cell links together. If you have small manipulative blocks which link together in a honeycomb design, show the blocks as a larger model of the honeycomb.
3. If you are able to secure an old beehive from the woods, cut it open on one side, leaving the other side intact. Compare what you see to the honeycomb in the jar of honey.
4. If you have a beekeeper in the community, ask that person to bring in a beehive without the bees and explain how it works.
5. Serve toast and honey for snack.

## Teaching tips

Often naturalists with the local park service and nature centers will bring beehive exhibits to schools.

★ STORY S-T-R-E-T-C-H-E-R-S

# Your Own Animal Book

*This activity helps you and the children develop a school animal guide so that you can more completely explore your own world of animals. This guide becomes an ongoing activity as seasons change and new animals come and go.*

## Words to use

| | |
|---|---|
| migrate | field guide |
| animal names | identify |
| season names | observe |
| adult | observation |
| young | creature |
| nest | characteristic |

## Materials

animal pictures and magazines
a scrap book
animal field guides
binoculars
collecting jars and nets are nice additions for more in-depth study
You can write to your state Department of Conservation, The Audobon Society or The National Wildlife Federation for pictures and information on different species of animals

## What to do

1. Plan a field trip to observe animals in the school yard.
2. Once observed, the teacher should make a definite identification of the critter with the help of the children. Observe and discuss the obvious characteristics such as type of animal, color and size. Find it in the appropriate field guide, again with their help. You may have children who can readily identify some creatures. Your response might then be, "Hey, I bet you're right. Let's look it up and see what our book can tell us about it."
3. It is now time to make a book page for your find. This page should include a photo or accurate drawing so the children will be able to use it for future identification. It might also include "field sketches" by the children. Once a picture page has been made, the children can add materials that might come from the animal such as feathers or fur, written information on their own observations or snapshots. The page should be as personalized as possible so that it is a real reflection of the children's experience.
4. Remember this is an ongoing project. New animals come and go and the key to this activity is that it is never done. This encourages you and your children always to be looking for new visitors to the school, whether they be ants, snails, bluebirds or butterflies, and adding to your own animal book.

## Want to do more?

Collect an animal and keep it in the classroom to observe it for a long time; insects, small rodents, reptiles and fish are easily kept. Select an animal of the month. Try to find the state animal, insect, bird, etc. and observe them. Tape record the sounds of your critter. Discuss what the animals eat. Where do you find most critters, indoors or out-of-doors? Make a similar book for plants. If your setting is like most, a field guide to common weeds will be a big help.

★ MUDPIES TO MAGNETS

MAY

science activities

# Feather Race

**4+**

*This activity enhances children's critical thinking.*

## Words to use

fall
slowly
fast
race
first
last
drop

## Materials

1" piece of yarn or string
feathers
objects—tissue, penny, paper cups, cotton ball, paper clip, etc.
paper
crayons

## What to do

1. Attach the piece of yarn or string to two objects in the classroom so that it is about 3 feet above the floor. This creates a line.
2. Select two children to play.
3. One child uses the feather and the other child chooses an object from those listed above.
4. Each child drops the "racer" from the yarn line at the same time.
5. Keep a record of which object wins the race.

★ WHERE IS THUMBKIN?

# Turning Mudpies into Houses

**5+**

*In times long past, house builders throughout the world discovered that soil mixed with straw and water would, with the sun's help, harden into bricks. Aside from the fun of approved mud play, the children learn about evaporation, building construction and the creative use of natural resources.*

## Words to use

solid
liquid
evaporation
mix
mixture
adobe
straw
construct

## Materials

empty pint milk cartons trimmed to about 1" high
dirt (with clay base helps)
dried straw or grass from the yard
water
large tub for mixing

## What to do

1. In the mixing tub, mix the soil with the water until it is the consistency of pancake batter. Add the dried grass clippings or straw. It will pour better if the straw is cut into small pieces before mixing.
2. As you mix, talk about the importance of the water as a mixing agent and how dirt and water can each be poured. Why do you mix dirt and grass? The grass holds dirt together.
3. Where does the water go? Place a plastic quart bag over one carton of adobe. Water should collect at the top of the bag, showing it escaped the mud via evaporation.
4. Place a similar bag over another carton but don't completely cover it. No water should appear. Would adobe be a good way to build houses in your area? Why or why not?
5. After mixing, spoon the mixture into the milk cartons. Tamp the container so that the mud slides down. The surface of the brick will then be flat for later stacking.
6. Place the containers in the sun to bake and dry. This will take several days depending on the humidity. You may remove the bricks from the molds (cartons) as soon as the mixture sets, in order to reuse the containers.
7. Build a simple adobe construction using mud for your mortar. Plaster it with more mud to form smooth walls. Let it dry thoroughly before using for play.

## Want to do more?

Make concrete in the cartons using cement, gravel and water. The proper proportions for mixing should be listed on your bag of cement. This shows how water mixes with a solid to form another solid. Ice cubes can be frozen into blocks which can later, on a cold day (might be fun on a warm day too!), be turned into ice houses. In each of the block making activities, water is the key. The study of the three phases of matter can be related as the matter changes. You may make a house from each set of construction materials. For the adobe, a wet sponge can be used to smooth the stacked blocks to form a continuous wall. For an ice structure, you will need a day with temperatures around freezing and a wet sponge or sprayer filled with water to help form a solid structure from ice blocks. Concrete, like bricks, will require a mortar to keep things in place. Packing snow into milk containers would provide another building material.

★ MUDPIES TO MAGNETS

# Snack and Cooking Activities

## Clifford's Birthday Party                    3+

*Children learn to decorate a cake.*

### Words to use

party            cake
decorate         frosting
frost            icing

### Materials

*Clifford's Birthday Party* by Norman Bridwell
cake or cakes
frosting
spatulas
bowl of warm water
cans of different colored cake decorating icing
plates
napkins
glasses
forks
milk

### What to do

1. Bake the cake or cakes ahead of time.
2. Have some children frost the cake using spatulas. Dipping the spatulas in warm water helps the frosting spread more easily.
3. Let other children decorate the cake by using the cans of colored icing which spreads when they push on the nozzles.
4. Serve the cake at snack time with glasses or cartons of cold milk.
5. Sing "Happy Birthday" to Clifford.

### Teaching tips

Younger children find it easier to decorate long flat sheet cakes. Older children can help bake the cakes one day and decorate them on another. If you have parents or grandparents who decorate cakes for a hobby, ask them to come to class and show the children some of their special tricks and the special tools they use.

★ MORE STORY S-t-r-e-t-c-h-e-r-s

# Banana Delights

**3+**

*Children develop fine motor skills and hand-eye coordination.*

### Words to use

banana          peel
sweet           freeze
cold

### Materials

bananas
popsicle sticks
plastic knife

### What to do

1. The children peel the bananas.
2. Using the plastic knife, allow the children to cut the bananas in half.
3. Give one half to each child. Place the bananas on popsicle sticks.
4. Freeze the bananas.
5. Eat and enjoy.

★ WHERE IS THUMBKIN?

# Fresh Strawberries

**3+**

*Children learn to cap, wash and serve fresh strawberries.*

### Words to use

strawberries    red
fruit           sweet
juicy           snack

### Materials

a quart of strawberries
teaspoons
colander

### What to do

1. Demonstrate how to wash the strawberries under a gentle flow of tap water, then place them in a colander to drain.
2. Show the cooking and snack helpers how to remove the caps from the strawberries by using the edge of a teaspoon.
3. Let the helpers serve the strawberries to their classmates during snack time.

## Teaching tips

Serve the fresh strawberries, then taste frozen ones, strawberry jam and preserves.

★ MORE STORY S-T-R-E-T-C-H-E-R-S

# No Cooking Picnic                               3+

*Children prepare a "no-cooking" picnic.*

## Words to use

picnic
lunch
basket
tablecloth
pack
snack
blanket
outside

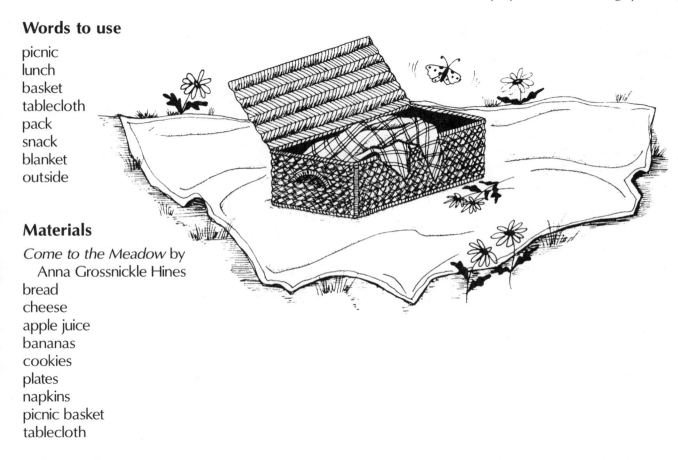

## Materials

*Come to the Meadow* by
   Anna Grossnickle Hines
bread
cheese
apple juice
bananas
cookies
plates
napkins
picnic basket
tablecloth

## What to do

1. Have some children assist you in packing a picnic lunch like Mattie's and Grandmother's.
2. Since all these items would be too much for one snack, cut the sandwiches and bananas into bite-sized pieces. Plan for a cup of juice and a whole cookie per child.
3. Serve snack outside on a picnic tablecloth.

## Teaching tips

Have the picnic basket nearby for any beautiful day when snacking outside would be a treat. The spontaneity of a picnic cheers teachers and children.

★ STORY S-T-R-E-T-C-H-E-R-S

# Ants on a Log                                                   3+

*Children learn to make a tasty snack.*

**Words to use**

celery
peanut butter
raisins
log
ants

**Materials**

celery
peanut butter
raisins

**What to do**

1. The children spread peanut butter on celery to create a log.
2. Place raisins on the peanut butter to look like ants.
3. Yum!

★ WHERE IS THUMBKIN?

# Raw Carrot Crunch                                              3+

*Children learn to use a vegetable peeler.*

**Words to use**

carrot
crunch
peel
cut
snack

**Materials**

carrots
several vegetable peelers
two paring knives
small cutting boards, if possible
small bowls

**What to do**

1. Ask a few children to help wash the carrots.
2. Demonstrate how to use a vegetable peeler.
3. Allow the children to scrape the outside of the carrots.

4. Assist them in slicing the carrots. Have only two paring knives used at once so that you can supervise.
5. Prepare enough raw carrots for snack time.

## Teaching tips

Try to find the carrots which are not packaged and still have their green tops because many children are not used to seeing them. Describe how the carrots grow with the greens on top of the ground and the carrot underneath the ground.

★ Story S-t-r-e-t-c-h-e-r-s

# Peter Rabbit's Salad                           3+

*Children learn to prepare fresh vegetables for a salad.*

## Words to use

vegetables
salad
mix
label

## Materials

*The Tale of Peter Rabbit* by Beatrix Potter
lettuce
carrots
radishes
French beans or green beans
parsley
colander
vegetable peeler
paring knife
paper towels
salad plates or bowls
masking tape
marker
napkins
forks

## What to do

1. On a day when you read *The Tale of Peter Rabbit,* let each child prepare his or her own salad.
2. Ask the helpers to set up the vegetables, wash the lettuce and place it into the colander to drain.
3. Place the salads in an area where they will be out of the way until all the children have theirs prepared. Make a label from a strip of masking tape and print the child's name on the label to identify their salads.
4. Eat Peter Rabbit's Salads at snack time.

## Teaching tips

If possible, have a few children go with the teacher's aide or the center director or school principal to shop for the vegetables for Peter Rabbit's Salad.

★ More Story S-t-r-e-t-c-h-e-r-s

# Pretzel Letters

**3+**

*Children learn about letters in this hands-on, yummy activity.*

## Words to use

names
letter
mix
dough
form
shape

## Materials

water
1-1/2 cups flour
1 envelope yeast
1 teaspoon salt
bowl and mixing spoon
egg
small bowl
fork
baking sheet

## What to do

1. Prepare pretzel dough. Mix the following ingredients.

> *1-1/2 cups warm water*
> *4 cups flour*
> *1 envelope of yeast*
> *1 teaspoon salt*

2. Give each child enough dough to shape into the first letter of his or her name.
3. Brush dough letters with beaten egg and sprinkle with coarse salt.
4. Bake at 425°F for twelve minutes.

★ The Instant Curriculum

# Tea Party Day

*Children learn how to be good hosts and hostesses.*

## Words to use

tea party
guest
invitation
tablecloth
candle
candlestick
cookies
tea
flowers

## Materials

paper and markers or
   crayons
tablecloths
flowers and candle,
   optional
cookies
"tea" (juice)
plates and cups

## What to do

1. Have each child design his own invitation to a tea party to take home to his parents inviting them to tea.
2. Invite the support staff to your tea party.
3. Use tablecloths on the tables and a floral centerpiece or candles in candlesticks.
4. Teachers and children all dress up for school and bring their guests.
5. Children serve "tea" and cookies to their guests.
6. We have had a tea party for several years and it is one of our most enjoyable activities.

★ ThemeStorming

## The Caterpillar                                    3+

*Help children get ready for a story or group activity with this poem. The metamorphosis of a caterpillar into a butterfly is introduced with this fingerplay.*

### Words to use

caterpillar
cocoon
asleep
creep
butterfly

### Materials

### What to do

1. Hold up an index finger.
2. Wiggle it while saying, "Show me your caterpillar."
3. Begin the rhyme.

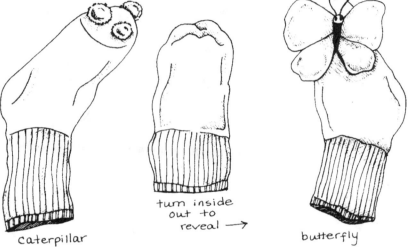

caterpillar

turn inside out to reveal →

butterfly

*A caterpillar crawled (hold left hand in air and slowly wiggle right index finger up)*
*To the top of a tree.*
*"I think I'll take a nap,"*
*Said he.*
*So under a leaf (crawl right index finger to palm of left hand)*
*He began to creep.*
*He spun a cocoon*
*And he fell asleep.*
*For six long months*
*He slept in that cocoon bed.*
*Till spring came along*
*And said, "Wake up. (shake hand)*
*Wake up, you sleepy head."*
*Out of the leaf (clasp thumbs together and flutter fingers like a butterfly)*
*He began to creep.*
*And he did cry,*
*"Lo, I am a butterfly!"*

## Want to do more?

With an old sock, some pompoms and felt, make a magic caterpillar as a prop. On the outside of the sock, glue three pompoms to look like eyes and a mouth. Turn the sock inside out and sew a felt butterfly on the inside. To start the poem, show the sock caterpillar, pull the top of the sock over the toe and dangle it to look like the cocoon (or chrysalis), then poke the inside out to reveal the butterfly.

★ TRANSITION TIME

# Pretty Butterfly                                                            3+

*Pretty Butterfly sparks children's interest and helps them settle down in a positive way.*

## Words to use

butterfly
fly
shoulder
tummy
toes
head
bed
softly

## Materials

## What to do

1. Clasp thumbs together and flutter fingers around like a butterfly while singing the following song to the tune of "Twinkle, Twinkle, Little Star."
2. Let the children watch at first, then encourage them to follow along.

> *Pretty, pretty butterfly (flutter hands like a butterfly)*
> *Flying up in the sky.*
> *Pretty, pretty butterfly,*
> *Fly, fly, fly, fly.*
> *Light upon my shoulder, (place butterfly on shoulders, then nose)*
> *Then upon my nose.*
> *Light upon my tummy, (place butterfly on tummy, then toes)*
> *Then upon my toes.*
> *Pretty, pretty butterfly (flutter hands, then place on head)*
> *Light upon my head.*
> *Pretty, pretty butterfly (put hands in lap)*
> *Go to bed.*

3. Now that you have the children's attention, lower your voice and talk softly so you don't wake the butterflies.

**Want to do more?**

Let the children make a butterfly to use as they sing this song. Give each child a sandwich baggie, some tissue paper and a pipe cleaner. Let him tear up the tissue paper and put it in the baggie. Tuck in the end of the plastic bag, then wrap the pipe cleaner around it to make a body and antennae. Attach a piece of yarn for flying.

★ TRANSITION TIME

# Cluck-Cluck Cup                                                     3+

*The children's curiosity about this "clucking cup" will help you gather them for a group activity. As children try to discover how the strange sound is made, they will be exercising scientific methods!*

### Words to use

| cluck | squeak |
|-------|--------|
| noise | string |
| wet   |        |

What is making that sound?

### Materials

| plastic cup | 18" string |
|-------------|------------|
| scissors    | paper clip |
| water       |            |

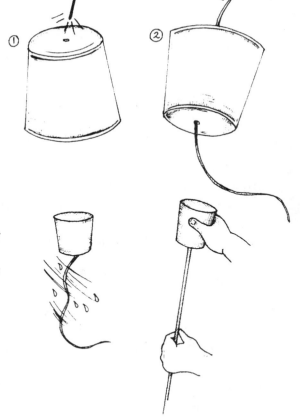

### What to do

1. Poke a hole in the bottom of the cup with the point of the scissors or a nail.
2. Thread the string through the hole and tie the paper clip to the end of the string in the cup.
3. Wet the string, hold the cup in one hand, and tightly pull down on the string with the other hand.
4. The string should make a squeaky, clucking sound. (Use more water and pull in jerky movements if it doesn't work.)
5. As children come over to see what the noise is, ask them open-ended questions about what is making the sound.

### Want to do more?

Try making other unusual sounds to get children's attention, or use musical instruments or a music box.

★ TRANSITION TIME

# Center Cards

**3+**

*Center Cards help children follow directions and give them an opportunity to experience an area of the room they might not choose on their own.*

## Words to use

centers

play

choose

activities

new

card

## Materials

school supply catalog or markers and crayons

poster board cut into 4″ x 6″ rectangles

scissors

glue

## What to do

1. Draw or cut out pictures representing various centers or activities. Make the number of pictures for each center match the number of children who can play in that area. For example, cut out two pictures of a sand or water table, four of blocks, two for easel painting, etc.
2. Glue the pictures to the poster board pieces.
3. Mix up the cards and turn them over so the pictures are face down.
4. Let one child at a time come up and choose a card.
5. Although children are usually allowed to make their own choices, use Center Cards occasionally to provide variety and new direction.

## Want to do more?

Play "show me" with the Center Cards. Have children match up the pictures on the cards with real objects in the classroom.

★ Transition Time

# The Number Game

**4+**

*This activity teaches children numeral recognition.*

## Words to use

number

numeral

step

wave

hold up

## Materials

large cards with the numerals 1-10 on them

## What to do

1. Give each of the children a number card.
2. Sing the following song and ask the children who are holding the cards with the numbers identified in the song to follow the song's directions.

> *"Number Song"*
>
> *The one steps in.*
> *The one steps out.*
> *The one holds up his number.*
> *And he waves it all about.*
> *The one brings me his number*
> *Then goes to wash his hands. (or goes to another activity)*
> *Where is the two?*
> *The two steps in*
> *The two steps out....*

3. Sing the numbers in order and repeat until all the children have a turn.

## Want to do more?

**Language**: Give each child a sheet of paper that has a numeral written on it and ask the children to draw or paste that number of items on a sheet. Compile the sheets to make a class number book.

## Songs to sing

"Five Little Ducks Went Out to Play"
"Seven Little Rabbits"
"Three Monkeys Swinging in a Tree"

## Books to read

*I Can Count* by Dick Bruna
*Seven Little Rabbits* by John Becker
*Ten Apples Up On Top* by Theo LeSieg
*Ten in the Bed* by Penny Dale
*You Can Name 100 Dinosaurs* by Randy Chewning

★ THE GIANT ENCYCLOPEDIA OF CIRCLE TIME AND GROUP ACTIVITIES

MAY

transition activities

# Double the Fun (or How to Find a Partner)     3+

*Many activities for children involve working in groups of two. Left free to pick their own partner, children who tend to be exclusive in their choices will limit their opportunities to relate to others. Here are two methods that use chance to form partnerships among children.*

## Words to use

partner
cooperate

## Materials

4' lengths of yarn, all the same color, one length for each pair of children
   or
pairs of identical (in shape and color) construction paper for each pair of children

## What to do

1. Untangling yarn: Arrange the lengths of yarn side by side. Gather the ends so that they protrude about four inches from your hand. Ask each child to select one end from one string of yarn. When you let go, challenge the children to unravel the strings without letting go of the end in their hand. Can they find their partner at the other end of the string?
2. Matching shapes and colors: Take each pair of construction paper shapes and shuffle them with all the other pairs. Distribute one cutout to each child. When all are distributed, ask the children to find the one that matches theirs. This person will be their partner.
3. If there is an odd number of children, join in the activity. If not, help where needed.

## Want to do more?

To make the yarn activity more difficult, overlap the lengths back and forth before the children try to unravel the yarn. Matching shapes can be made more difficult by reducing the number of colors and making the shapes more complex or more similar.

## Home connection

Many of the activities you suggest to parents involve children and adults working together as partners. "Double the Fun" could be tried at home as a fun way to find a partner.

★ THE PEACEFUL CLASSROOM

# The Birthday Train                                           3+

*Encourages children's creative thinking.*

## Words to use

circle
train
birthday
chant
aboard

## Materials

## What to do

1. Ask the children to form a circle.
2. Take the hand of one child.
3. Walk around the inside of the circle with that child as everyone chants,

> *Come aboard the birthday train,*
> *Come aboard the birthday train.*
> *What do you want for your birthday?*
> *Come aboard the birthday train.*

4. Pause in front of one child.
5. Ask him to say what he wants for his birthday.
6. After he does, ask him to join the train.
7. Continue chanting the verse until all the children have had a turn to tell what they want for their birthday.
8. When the game ends, there will be one large birthday train!

★ 500 Five Minute Games

# Ticklers                                                      3+

*This activity encourages cooperation, learning how to take turns and just plain fun.*

## Words to use

stomach
laugh
ha ha
describe

## Materials

## What to do

1. Have children lie on the floor on their backs with each child placing her head on another child's stomach.
2. Tell the children to laugh.
3. Let each child describe how it felt when everyone was laughing.

★ The Instant Curriculum

# Guessing Game                                    3+

*This activity develops children's thinking skills.*

## Words to use

guess
describe
chant

## Materials

small bag with drawstring
small pictures of animals (pictures of animals can be cut from magazines and laminated for durability)

## What to do

1. Put the pictures of animals in the bag.
2. Shake the bag and say the following chant.

> *Bag, oh bag*
> *Shake, shake, shake.*
> *Bag, oh bag*
> *What shall I take?*

3. Take one animal out of the bag and hide it in your hand.
4. Describe the animal to a child until he or she guesses what animal it is.
5. Give the picture of the animal to the child to hold.
6. Continue until all children have a chance to play.
Note: Use pictures of familiar animals, but if the chosen child cannot guess the animal, ask other children to help.

## Want to do more?

**Language**: Use pictures relating to a theme (trees, plants, flowers, insects). When children understand how to describe the pictures, let them have a turn to shake and choose a child to guess the animal.

★ The Giant Encyclopedia of Circle Time and Group Activities

MAY

games

# Busy Bees

3+

*Teaches children body awareness.*

**Words to use**

bee
buzz
fly
touch
parts of the body

**Materials**

**What to do**

1. Ask the children to move around the room saying "bzzz, bzzz, bzzz," pretending to be bees.
2. Call out the name of a part of the body, like elbows.
3. The children stop and gently touch their elbows to another child's elbow.

★ 500 FIVE MINUTE GAMES

# Fuzzy Wuzzy Caterpillar

3+

*Teaches about butterflies.*

**Words to use**

caterpillar
fuzzy
blanket
sleep
wings
butterfly

**Materials**

MAY

games

## What to do

Act out the following poem with the children.

> *Fuzzy wuzzy caterpillar,*
> *Into a corner crept.*
> *Spun around himself a blanket,*
> *And for a long time slept. (curl up and pretend to sleep)*
> *Roly-poly caterpillar,*
> *Wakening by and by,*
> *Found himself with beautiful wings,*
> *Changed to a butterfly. (fly around the room with arms spread)*

★ 500 Five Minute Games

# Five Little Children                3+

*Develops children's rhyming, thinking and counting skills.*

## Words to use

rhyme
sounds like
missing
fill in
four
three
two
one

## Materials

## What to do

Recite the following poem with the children and let them fill in the missing words.

> *Five little children playing on the shore,*
> *One went away and then there were _____.*
> *Four little children sailing on the sea,*
> *One went away and then there were _____.*
> *Three little children mixing up a stew,*
> *One stopped stirring and then there were _____.*
> *Two little children playing in the sun,*
> *One went home and then there was _____.*
> *One little child playing all alone,*
> *Went to talk to friends on the telephone. (pretend to pick up a*
> *phone and talk)*

★ 500 Five Minute Games

# Goldilocks

*Teaches children sequencing skills.*

## Words to use

beginning
middle
end
house
huge
small
tiny
too big
too small
just right

## Materials

## What to do

1. Recite the following poem with the children.

> *When Goldilocks went to the three bears' house*
> *What did her blue eyes see?*
> *A bowl that was huge, (make a large circle with arms)*
> *A bowl that was small, (make a smaller circle with arms)*
> *A bowl that was teeny and that was all. (make a circle with fingers)*
> *She counted them one, two, three. (hold up three fingers one at a time)*

2. Continue with:

> *When Goldilocks went to the three bears' house...*
> *A chair that was huge...*

> *When Goldilocks went to the three bears' house...*
> *A bed that was huge...*

> *When Goldilocks went to the three bears' house...*
> *A bear that was huge...*

★ 500 FIVE MINUTE GAMES

# Hoop Golf

**4+**

*This may help younger children recognize numerals and learn their sequence. They will also practice throwing in a controlled way. School-age children can practice addition skills and satisfy their need to compete in a way that gives a chance for success to most children.*

## Words to use

hoop
beanbag
throw
target
course
one
two
three
four
five

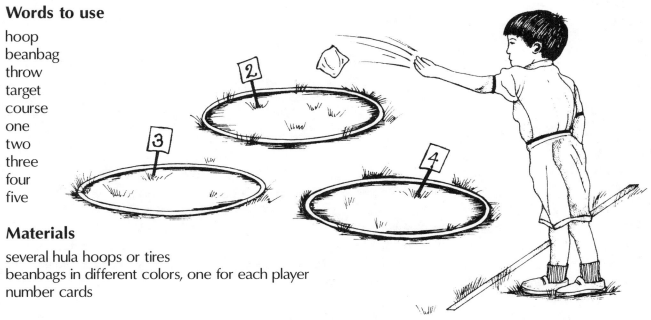

## Materials

several hula hoops or tires
beanbags in different colors, one for each player
number cards

## What to do

1. Place the hoops or tires at various spots on the playground to make a "course." Put the number one card in the first hoop, the number two in the second hoop and so on.
2. Create a starting line ten feet or more from the first hoop.
3. The first child stands behind the starting line and tries to throw her beanbag into the first hoop.
4. Count how many throws it takes her to get the beanbag to land in the hoop. Write down the number of throws for each child on a separate score sheet.
5. The child then stands inside the first hoop and throws her beanbag toward the second hoop, again keeping track of the number of throws. Continue until the child has thrown her beanbag in the last hoop. Add up the score.

## Want to do more?

For younger children, score keeping is totally unnecessary. They will simply enjoy throwing the bean bag from one hoop to another. To make the game easier, bring the hoops closer together. To add difficulty, increase the distance and the number of hoops. Once they know the game well, let the children set the course and devise their own variations.

★ THE OUTSIDE PLAY AND LEARNING BOOK

# Barnyard

**4+**

*This is an exercise in "auditory discrimination." The child must listen for one particular sound among many other distracting sounds.*

### Words to use

| | |
|---|---|
| listen | animal sounds |
| duck | pig |
| cow | dog |
| cat | group |

### Materials

a large group of children

### What to do

1. Think of three animals that make interesting sounds, such as a duck, a pig and a cow.
2. Whisper one of the three animal names into the ear of each child playing the game.
3. The children scatter around the playground.
4. At a signal from you, all the children start making the sound of their animal. As they continue to make the noises, they try to find all the other children of their own "species" who are making the same noise, eventually gathering into three noisy groups.

### Want to do more?

Vary the animals from day to day. Older children and adults could be told to close their eyes while they search for their species. In this case, you will need "guards" with their eyes open to keep people from bumping into others or wandering out of the area.

★ THE OUTSIDE PLAY AND LEARNING BOOK

# One Finger

**4+**

*Develops children's coordination.*

### Words to use

finger
thumb
arm
leg
nod of the head
stand up
sit down
turn around
keep moving

## Materials

## What to do

1. This is a popular song that children enjoy very much.
2. If you don't know the melody, saying the words is just as much fun.
3. Start the song quietly, while sitting down.
4. The actions build up with each verse. Keep in constant motion throughout the song.

> *One finger, one thumb, keep moving*
> *One finger, one thumb, keep moving*
> *One finger, one thumb, keep moving*
> *And we'll all be merry and bright.*
>
> *One finger, one thumb, one arm, keep moving...*
> *One finger, one thumb, one arm, one leg, keep moving...*
> *One finger, one thumb, one arm, one leg, one nod of the head, keep moving...*
> *One finger, one thumb, one arm, one leg, one nod of the head, stand up, sit*
> *    down, keep moving...*
> *One finger, one thumb, one arm, one leg, one nod of the head, stand up, sit*
> *    down, turn around, keep moving...*

5. Make up as many additional actions as you wish.

★ 500 Five Minute Games

# Seeing I's                                                     4+

*This activity adds more uncertainty to the experience of wearing a blindfold. Wearers will have to be patient while their helpers provide them with objects to explore. Children will have the opportunity to both receive and give assistance.*

## Words to use

help
blind
senses
sight
touch
smell
hear
give
pretend

## Materials

one small paper sack and one blindfold for every pair of children

## What to do

1. Tell the children you have a kindness activity involving a blindfold for them to try. One child will wear the blindfold while his partner finds things for him to feel, hear and smell.
2. Ask each child to find a partner. Give the pair a blindfold and a paper bag. Ask them who will be the helper and who will wear the blindfold.
3. Ask the helpers to find four interesting objects for their blindfolded partners to feel, hear and smell. Ask them to put the objects into the bag and keep what they select a secret.
4. When they return, help them put the blindfold on their partners. When the children are ready, the helpers can open the bags and give one object to the child to explore. After about 30 seconds, tell them they can hand over the next thing they found.
5. To reduce distraction, discourage the children from talking too much during the activity.
6. When all the objects have been shared, the children can reverse roles.

## Want to do more?

Show the children how to hand something gently to someone who cannot see. Blindfolded children can be startled by a partner who drops objects into their hands. Emphasize the idea that sometimes people do not want help. Blind people, for example, learn to explore the world and find things on their own. Avoid creating the impression that handicapped people are completely dependent on others. To simplify the activity, prepare bags ahead of time with three or four items for children to hand to their partners.

## Home connection

Parents can repeat the activity with their children at home, taking turns being the helper.

★ THE PEACEFUL CLASSROOM

# Books

*I Is One* by Tasha Tudor
*Across the Stream* by Mirra Ginsburg
*A Letter to Amy* by Ezra Jack Keats
*Animals Should Definitely Not Act Like People* by Judi Barrett
*Animals Should Definitely Not Wear Clothing* by Judi Barrett
*Anno's Alphabet* by Anno Mitsmasa
*Baby Animals* by Margaret Wise Brown
*Birthday Presents* by Cynthia Rylant
*Caps for Sale* by Esphyr Slobodkina
*Clifford's Birthday Party* by Norman Bridwell
*Come to the Meadow* by Anna Grossnickle Hines
*Count and See* by Tana Hoban
*Counting Sheep* by John Archambault
*Curious George* by H.A. Rey
*Dabble Duck* by Anne L. Ellis
*Dr. Seuss ABC's* by Dr. Seuss
*Five Little Ducks* by Raffi
*Five Little Monkeys* by Eileen Christelow
*Follow Me!* by Mordicai Gerstein
*Hand, Hand, Fingers, Thumb* by Al Perkins
*I Wish That I Had Duck Feet* by Theo LeSieg
*Make Way for Ducklings* by Robert McCloskey
*The Monkey and the Crocodile* by Paul Galdone
*One, Two, One Pair* by Bruce McMillan
*One Two Three: An Animal Counting Book* by Marc Brown
*On Market Street* by Arnold Lobel
*Ten Black Dots* by Donald Crews
*The Birthday Thing* by SuAnn Kiser and Kevin Kiser
*The Tale of Peter Rabbit* by Beatrix Potter
*The Ugly Duckling* by Hans Christian Anderson
*The Very Hungry Caterpillar* by Eric Carle
*Three Little Ducks Went Wandering* by Ron Roy
*Where Butterflies Grow* by Joanne Ryder
*Where Can It Be?* by Ann Jonas
*Wild Wild Sunflower Child Anna* by Nancy White Carlstrom

# Records, Tapes and CDs

Beall, Pamela Conn and Susan Hagen Nipp. "The Ants Go Marching" from *Wee Sing Silly Songs.* Price Stern Sloan, 1986.

Beall, Pamela Conn and Susan Hagen Nipp. "Three Little Monkeys" from *Wee Sing Children's Songs and Fingerplays.* Price Stern Sloan, 1979.

Hammett, Carol Totsky and Elaine Bueffel, "Six White Ducks" from *Toddlers on Parade.* Kimbo, 1985.

Palmer, Hap. "Ants" from *Pretend.* Educational Activities.

Palmer, Hap. *Mod Marchers.* Activity Records, 1965.

Raffi. "Six White Ducks" from *More Singable Songs.* A and M Records.

Sharon, Lois and Bram. "Five Little Monkeys" from *One Elephant, Deux Elephants.* Elephant Records, 1978.

Sharon, Lois and Bram. "Three Little Monkeys" from *Smorgasbord.* Elephant Records, 1980.

# Spring Activities Listed by Source

## 500 Five Minute Games

**March**—Guess the Song; The Little Toad; The March Wind; Margery Daw; Move That Air!, Nursery Rhyme Game

**April**—It Rained a Mist; Make a Rainbow; Partner Moves; Plant a Little Seed; Rain Poem; Rain Sayings; Twiddle Your Thumbs; Seeds

**May**—The Birthday Train; Busy Bees; Five Little Children; Fuzzy Wuzzy Caterpillar; Goldilocks; Hot Letters; One Finger; Slowly, Slowly

## The Complete Learning Center Book

**March**—Building a Car; Colonial Hat; Fancy Hats; Gas Station and Garage Center; Hat Center; Three-Cornered Hat; Transportation; Whose Hat Is This?

**April**—Changing Colors; Designing a Flower Garden; Gardening Apron; Greenhouse Center; I Found It; Sensory Center; Tasty Treats; Those That Are Alike

**May**—Fancy Clothes; Party Center; Pet Center; A Pet Show; Scavenger Hunt

## Earthways

**March**—Pinwheels; Round Wind Wands

**May**—Butterfly Pop-up Cards; Flower or Leafy Crowns; Pressed Flower Cards; Tissue Paper Butterflies and Mobiles

## The GIANT Encyclopedia of Circle Time and Group Activities

**March**—Humpty Dumpty; Miss and Mr. Muffet; Roll a Rhyme

**April**—I'm Listening to the Rain; A Little Sun; Seed to Flower Rhyme Play; Sing a Song of Spring; What a Storm!

**May**—Do Things Four Times; Guessing Game; The Number Game; My Favorite Stuffed Friend; Our Class Alphabet; Ribbons and Bows; We Are the Number Train

## The GIANT Encyclopedia of Theme Activities

**March**—Jack and Jill; Let's Be the Wind; Spring Cleaning; Spring Mud Painting; To Move or Not to Move; Wind-o-Meter; Wind Sock

**April**—Dirt Day; Flower Colors Match Up; Puddle Game; Robin; Seed Wheel; What's in a Bird's Nest?

**May**—Bumble Bee; Buzz, Buzz; It's an Animal

## Hug a Tree

**March**—Measure Shadows

**April**—What Color Is Spring?

**May**—1, 2, 3, Hush

## The Instant Curriculum

**March**—Around the Chairs; Billy Goats Gruff; Car Wash; Drive-In; Good Graffiti; Imagination Chair; Mad Hatters; Magic Wand; Positional Words; Rebus Charts; Straw Blowing; Writing Rhymes

**April**—Circle Songs; Crunchy Sets; Divided Singing; Egg Carton Shake; Match Makers; Pen Pals; Pick a Pair; Preschool Fitness; Puppet Party; Target Practice; Two Feet Long; Walking in the Rain; Window Garden

**May**—Butterfly Wings; Creepy Caterpillars; Lacing Letter; Lucky Letters; On Stage; Pretzel Letters; Sand Letters; Slinky Letters; Ticklers

## The Learning Circle

**March**—Spring Hunt; Spring Mural

**April**—Build a Bird's Nest; Plant Brainstorms

## More Mudpies to Magnets

**March**—Air Resistance Race; Balloon Fliers; Jumping on Air; Make Your Own Greenhouse; Streamers

**April**—A House for Snugs (short for Snails and Slugs); The House of Worms

**May**—On the Trail of Fives

## More Story S-t-r-e-t-c-h-e-r-s

**March**—Blueberry Muffins; Cheese and Crackers

**April**—Book of Our Favorite Spring Flowers and Birds; Gardening; Gardening Clothes; Harold's Purple Fruits; Listening for Birds; Painting Spring Flower; Picnic on a Lovely Spring Day; Seed and Gardening Catalogs; Spring Flower Puzzles; Water Drop Splash Prints; Yellow Rain Slickers and Other Rain Wear

**May**—Animal Antics; Clifford's Birthday Party; Fresh Strawberries; From Egg to Caterpillar to Pupa to Butterfly; Making Party Hats; Party Piñata; Peter Rabbit's Salad; Peter Rabbit, Where Are You?; Pet Supply Store; Torn Paper Collage Animals; Whose Baby Am I?

## Mudpies to Magnets

**March**—Twig Race

**April**—Dance a Garden; Puddle Walk; Rainbow in a Jar; Seed Power

**May**—Turning Mudpies into Houses; Your Own Animal Book

## One Potato, Two Potato, Three Potato, Four

**March**—Humpty Dumpty; I Know a Little Pussy; Little Boy Blue

**April**—Doctor Foster; It's Raining; It's Pouring; One Misty, Moisty Morning; Rain on the Green Grass

**May**—One, Two, Buckle My Shoe; One, Two, Three, Four; There Were Five in the Bed

## The Outside Play and Learning Book

**March**—Frozen Nature Collages
**April**—Balls; Simple Sundial; Wheelbarrow or Wagon Gardens
**May**—Barnyard; Drawing in the Sand; Hoop Golf; Jump Ropes; Miniature Worlds; Pouring Experiments; Treasure Hunt for Golden Pebbles; What Shape Comes Next?; Who's Got More?

## The Peaceful Classroom

**March**—Adopt a Tree
**April**—Class Garden; Growing Flowers; Plant Life; School Garden
**May**—Back Stand; Double the Fun (or How to Find a Partner); Know Talk; Seeing I's

## Preschool Art

**March**—Bonnets; Paper Bag Kite; Paper Dolls; Plaster Bag Art
**April**—Batik Eggs; Chalk Flowers; Egg Paint; Eggshell Mosaic; Marbling; Onion Skin Egg; Walking Puppets
**May**—Claydoh Beads; Fence Weaving; Glitter Paint Shake; Shadow Drawing

## Story S-t-r-e-t-c-h-e-r-s

March—Breakfast Muffins
April—Carrot and Raisin Salad; Magnetic Numerals with Rhymes; The Parts of a Tree
May—Fireflies; Five Lost; Hives and Honeycombs; No Cooking Picnic; Pretend Picnic; Raw Carrot Crunch; Shape That Clay; Would You Let a Caterpillar Crawl on Your Hand?

## ThemeStorming

**May**—Tea Party Day

## Transition Time

**March**—Buddy Bunny; Five Little Kites; Journals; Note Tote; A Sailor Went to Sea; Story Headbands; Storyteller's Chair; Take Home Kits
**April**—Baby Birds; Early Risers; Five Little Birdies; Make Rain

## Transition Time

**May**—The Caterpillar; Center Cards; Cluck-Cluck Cup; Five Little Ducks; Pretty Butterfly

## Where Is Thumbkin?

**March**—Bakery; Big and Little Lambs; Can You Tell by Looking?; Falling Down; Hard and Soft; I'm a Little Teapot; Jack and Jill; Key Match; London Bridge; Mary Had a Little Lamb; Muffin Holder Flowers; Muffin Man; Muffin Patterns; Tall and Short; Tea Cup Match; Tea Party; Walking the Bridge; Walk Like a Lamb
**April**—Arm and Hand Tree; Bird's Nest; Eensy Weensy Spider; Egg Carton Gardens; Elephant Patterns; Feeding the Elephant; Gelatin Rainbows; The Green Grass Grows All Around; Green Snacks; Heavy/Light; One Elephant; Moving Like Elephants (formerly One Elephant); Over in the Meadow; Rainbows; Raindrop Close-ups; Rain, Rain; Scientific Observations; Spider Dance; Spider Puppets
**May**—The Ants Go Marching; Ants on a Log; Banana Delights; Duck Pond; Feather Painting; Feather Race; Five Little Ducks; Monkey Mask; Monkey See, Monkey Do; Old Lady Puppet; Rhyming Words Match; Sequencing; Six White Ducks; There Was an Old Lady; Three Little Monkeys; Thumbprint Ants; Variations of Five

# Sample Rebus Chart
## Directions for Making Muffins

1. Preheat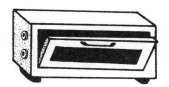

2. Place  in

3. Empty  into

4. Add 1 and ½ water

5. Stir

6. Pour into

7. Bake in

8. Serve and

# Steps in Binding a Book

 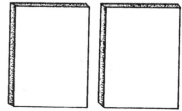 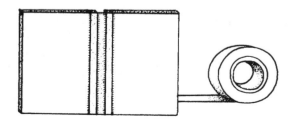

**1.** Cut two pieces of heavy cardboard slightly larger than the pages of the book.

**2.** With wide masking tape, tape the two pieces of cardboard together with ½-inch space between.

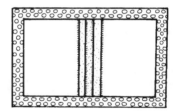  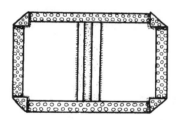

**3.** Cut outside cover 1½ inches larger than the cardboard and stick to cardboard (use thinned white glue if cover material is not self-adhesive.)

**4.** Fold corners over first, then the sides.

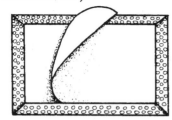 

**5.** Measure and cut inside cover material and apply as shown.

**6.** Place stapled pages of the book in the center of the cover. Secure with two strips of inside cover material, one at the front of the book and the other at the back.

# Spring Indexes

## Index of Terms

# Children's Book Index

# Recommended Titles

### Preschool Art
It's the Process, Not the Product

*MaryAnn Kohl*

Anyone working with preschoolers and early primary age children will want this book. Over 200 activities teach children to explore and understand their world through open-ended art experiences that emphasize the process of art, not the product. The first chapter introduces basic art activities appropriate for all children, while subsequent chapters, which build on the activities in the first chapter, are divided by seasons. With activities that include painting, drawing, collage, sculpture and construction, this is the only art book you will need. 260 pages. © 1994.

ISBN 0-87659-168-3
Gryphon House
16985
Paperback

### 500 Five Minute Games
Quick and Easy Activities for 3-6 Year Olds

*Jackie Silberg*

Enjoy five-minute fun with the newest book from the author who brought you the popular series Games to Play with Babies, Games to Play With Toddlers, and Games to Play With Two Year Olds. These games are easy, fun, developmentally appropriate, and promote learning in just five spare minutes of the day. Children unwind, get the giggles out, communicate, and build self-esteem as they have fun. Each game indicates the particular skill developed. 270 pages. © 1995.

ISBN 0-87659-172-1
Gryphon House
16455
Paperback

***Available at your favorite bookstore,
school supply store or order from Gryphon House®***

# Recommended Titles

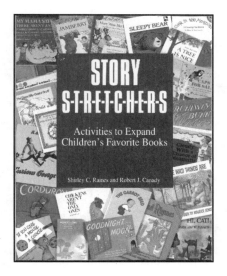

### Story S-t-r-e-t-c-h-e-r-s®:
Activities to Expand Children's Favorite Books (Pre-K and K)

*Shirley C. Raines and Robert J. Canady*

Here is a perfect way to connect children's enthusiasm for books with other areas of the curriculum. Using 450 ideas from children's best-loved picture books, children will experience exciting activities provided for a variety of learning centers in science, nature, math, movement and more. 256 pages. © 1989.

ISBN 0-87659-119-5
Gryphon House
10011
Paperback

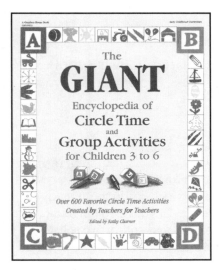

### The Giant Encyclopedia of Circle Time and Group Activities for Children 3 to 6
Over 600 Favorite Activities Created by Teachers for Teachers

*Edited by Kathy Charner*

Filled with over 600 activities covering 48 themes, this book is jam-packed with ideas that were tested by teachers in the classroom. Many activities include suggestions on integrating the circle time or group activity into other areas of the curriculum. 510 pages. © 1996.

ISBN 0-87659-181-0
Gryphon House
16413
Paperback

**Available at your favorite bookstore,
school supply store or order from Gryphon House®**

# Recommended Titles

### The Peaceful Classroom
162 Easy Activities to Teach Preschoolers Compassion and Cooperation

*Charles Smith, Ph.D*

Compassion, cooperation, friendship and respect for others are important to the development of every human being. The Peaceful Classroom is filled with appealing group learning activities which help children acquire these skills. The book also suggests ways teachers can work with parents to extend these learning experiences at home. A timely and important resource for every classroom. 208 pages. © 1993.

ISBN 0-87659-165-9
Gryphon House
15186
Paperback

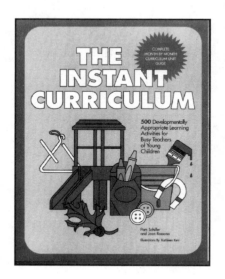

### The Instant Curriculum
500 Developmentally Appropriate Learning Activities for Busy Teachers of Young Children

*Pam Schiller and Joan Rossano*

With very little planning and preparation you can do 500 different developmentally appropriate learning activities with children. You can use activities by month or by subject. A few of the subjects included in these ready-to-use activities are art, fine and gross motor skills, language, math, music, problem-solving, dramatic play and imagination, and critical thinking. it's easy to find the right activity for any day or purpose. 390 pages. © 1990.

ISBN 0-87659-124-1
Gryphon House
10014
Paperback

***Available at your favorite bookstore,
school supply store or order from Gryphon House®***

# Recommended Titles

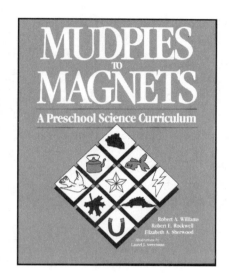

## Mudpies to Magnets
A Preschool Science Curriculum

*Elizabeth A. Sherwood, Robert A. Williams,*
*Robert E. Rockwell*

224 hands-on science experiments and ideas with step-by-step instructions delight and amaze children as they experience nature, the human body, electricity, floating and sinking and more. Children participate in ready-made projects such as making a tornado in a jar, creating constellations and growing crystals. Categorized by curriculum areas, each activity includes a list of vocabulary words. 157 pages. © 1987.

ISBN 0-87659-112-8
Gryphon House
10005
Paperback

## Where is Thumbkin?
500 Activities to Use with Songs You Already Know

Pam Schiller, Thomas Moore

These are the songs teachers and children are already singing together every day. The book is organized month-by-month, and has sections for toddlers, threes, fours, five and six year olds. These simple learning activities can be used in circle time, for transitions, or for special music time. A list of related children's literature and recordings accompanies each set of activities. 256 pages. © 1993.

ISBN 0-87659-164-0
Gryphon House
13156
Paperback

**Available at your favorite bookstore,**
**school supply store or order from Gryphon House®**